A Plain Account of
Christian Perfection

A Plain Account of
CHRISTIAN PERFECTION

*as believed and taught
by the Reverend Mr. John Wesley
from the year 1725 to the year 1777*

Reprinted from the complete original text
as authorized by the Wesleyan Conference
Office in London, England, in 1872.

BEACON HILL PRESS OF KANSAS CITY

Kansas City, Missouri

First Printing, Unabridged Edition, 1966

ISBN: 083-410-1580

15   14   13

Printed in United States of America

Preface

No statement of John Wesley's position on Christian perfection is more comprehensive or more truly representative of this great preacher's teachings on holiness than is his own *A Plain Account of Christian Perfection*. The text as here reproduced in its entirety is found in Volume IX of his complete works as compiled in 1872.

In diary-like form he reflects his deepening insights into the doctrine of holiness over the years from 1725 to 1777. As the editorial footnote on the original edition suggests, however: "It is not to be understood that Mr. Wesley's sentiments concerning Christian Perfection were in any measure changed after the year 1777. This tract underwent several revisions and enlargements during his lifetime. . . . The last revision appears to have been made in the year 1777." It is interesting to note the modifications in Wesley's original statements as reflected in his footnotes.

Incorporated in *Plain Account* are choice excerpts from major sermons and writings, and numerous quotations of hymns. The frequent use of the question-answer method to expound truth is perhaps the most unique characteristic of this work. The style is intimate and forthright, and the truth convincing.

The entire "tract" (as Wesley called it) is divided into 28 segments, some quite brief, others of considerable length. Wesley did not title the sections—merely numbered them—so to highlight the central ideas of each section, we have inserted a comprehensive title at the beginning of each and a brief outline for the larger ones.

All who desire a clearer understanding of the doctrine of Christian perfection will find immense value in this volume. Its rich spiritual insights will lift the soul of every earnest seeker after the deep things of God.

J. FRED PARKER
Book Editor

Contents

1

Statement of Purpose

What I purpose in the following papers, is, to give a plain and distinct account of the steps by which I was led, during a course of many years, to embrace the doctrine of Christian perfection. This I owe to the serious part of mankind, those who desire to know all "the truth as it is in Jesus." And these only are concerned in questions of this kind. To these I would nakedly declare the thing as it is, endeavoring all along to show, from one period to another, both what I thought, and why I thought so.

2

Importance of Complete Dedication

In the year 1725, being in the twenty-third year of my age, I met with Bishop Taylor's *Rule and Exercises of Holy Living and Dying.* In reading several parts of this book, I was exceedingly affected; that part in particular which relates to purity of intention. Instantly I resolved to dedicate all my life to God, all my thoughts and words, and actions; being thoroughly convinced, there was no medium; but that every part of my life (not some only) must either be a sacrifice to God, or myself, that is, in effect, to the devil.

Can any serious person doubt of this, or find a medium between serving God and serving the devil?

3

Simplicity of Intention

In the year 1726, I met with Kempis's "Christian's Pattern." The nature and extent of inward religion, the religion of the heart, now appeared to me in a stronger light than ever it had done before. I saw, that giving even all my life to God (supposing it possible to do this, and go no farther) would profit me nothing, unless I gave my heart, yea, all my heart to Him.

I saw, that "simplicity of intention, and purity of affection," one design in all we speak or do, and one desire ruling all our tempers, are indeed "the wings of the soul," without which she can never ascend to the mount of God.

4

No Half Christians

A year or two after, Mr. Law's *Christian Perfection* and *Serious Call* were put into my hands. These convinced me, more than ever, of the absolute impossibility of being half a Christian; and I determined, through His grace (the absolute necessity of which I was deeply sensible of), to be all devoted to God, to give Him all my soul, my body, and my substance.

Will any considerate man say, that this is carrying matters too far? or that anything less is due to Him who has given Himself for us, than to give Him ourselves, all we have, and all we are?

5

Conformity to the Master

In the year 1729, I began not only to read, but to study, the Bible as the one, the only standard of truth, and the only model of pure religion. Hence I saw, in a clearer and clearer light, the indispensable necessity of having "the mind which was in Christ," and of "walking as Christ also walked;" even of having, not some part only, but all the mind which was in Him; and of walking as He walked, not only in many or in most respects, but in all things. And this was the light, wherein at this time I generally considered religion, as a uniform following of Christ, an entire inward and outward conformity to our Master. Nor was I afraid of anything more, than of bending this rule to the experience of myself or of other men; of allowing myself in any the least disconformity to our grand Exemplar.

6

The Circumcision of the Heart

Cleansed from sin
Love, the fulfillment of the law
God must reign without a rival

On January 1, 1733, I preached before the university, in St. Mary's Church, on "The Circumcision of the Heart;" an account of which I gave in these words: "It is that habitual disposition of soul which, in the sacred writings, is termed holiness; and which directly implies the being cleansed from sin, 'from all filthiness both of flesh and spirit;' and, by consequence, the being endued with those virtues which were in Christ Jesus; the being so 'renewed in the image of our mind,' as to be 'perfect as our Father in heaven is perfect.' "— Vol. i, p. 148.

In the same sermon I observed, " 'Love is the fulfilling of the law, the end of the commandment,' It is not only 'the first and great' command, but all the commandments, in one. 'Whatsoever things are just, whatsoever things are pure, if there be any virtue, if there be any praise,' they are all comprised in this one word, love. In this is perfection, and glory, and happiness: the royal law of heaven and earth is this, 'Thou shalt love the Lord thy God with all thy heart, and with all thy soul, and with all thy mind, and with all thy strength.' The one perfect good shall be your one ultimate end. One thing shall ye desire for its own sake,— the fruition of Him who is all in all. One happiness shall ye propose to your souls, even a union with Him that made them, the having 'fellowship with the Father and the Son'; the being 'joined to the Lord in one Spirit.'

One design ye are to pursue to the end of time,—the enjoyment of God in time and in eternity. Desire other things, so far as they tend to this; love the creature, as it leads to the Creator. But in every step you take, be this the glorious point that terminates your view. Let every affection, and thought, and word, and action, be subordinate to this. Whatever ye desire or fear, whatever ye seek or shun, whatever ye think, speak, or do, be it in order to your hapiness in God, the sole end, as well as source, of your being."—*Ibid.*, pp. 150-51.

I concluded in these words: "Here is the sum of the perfect law, the circumcision of the heart. Let the spirit return to God that gave it, with the whole train of its affections. Other sacrifices from us He would not, but the living sacrifice of the heart hath He chosen. Let it be continually offered up to God through Christ, in flames of holy love. And let no creature be suffered to share with Him; for He is a jealous God. His throne will He not divide with another; He will reign without a rival. Be no design, no desire admitted there, but what has Him for its ultimate object. This is the way wherein those children of God once walked, who being dead still speak to us: 'Desire not to live but to praise His name; let all your thoughts, words, and works tend to His glory.' 'Let your soul be filled with so entire a love to Him, that you may love nothing but for His sake.' 'Have a pure intention of heart, a steadfast regard to His glory in all our actions.' 'For then, and not till then, is that mind in us, which was also in Christ Jesus when in every motion of our heart, in every word of our tongue, in every work of our hands, we pursue nothing but in relation to Him, and in subordination to His pleasure; when we too neither think, nor speak, nor act, to fulfil 'our own will, but the will of Him that sent us;' when, 'whether we eat or drink, or whatever we do,' we do it all 'to the glory of God.' "—*Ibid.*, p. 153.

It may be observed, this sermon was composed the

first of all my writings which have been published. This was the view of religion I then had, which even then I scrupled not to term *perfection*. This is the view I have of it now, without any material addition or diminution. And what is there here, which any man of understanding, who believes the Bible, can object to? What can he deny without flatly contradicting the Scripture? What retrench, without taking from the Word of God?

7

"Thy Pure Love Alone"

In the same sentiment did my brother and I remain (with all those young gentlemen in derision termed *Methodists*) till we embarked for America, in the latter end of 1735. It was the next year, while I was at Savannah, that I wrote the following lines: —

> *Is there a thing beneath the sun,*
> *That strives with Thee my heart to share?*
> *Ah! tear it thence, and reign alone,*
> *The Lord of every motion there!*

In the beginning of the year 1738, as I was returning from thence, the cry of my heart was,

> *O grant that nothing in my soul*
> *May dwell, but Thy pure love alone!*
> *O may Thy love possess me whole,*
> *My joy, my treasure, and my crown.*
> *Strange fires far from my heart remove—*
> *My every act, word, thought, be love!*

I never heard that anyone objected to this. And, indeed, who can object? Is not this the language, not only of every believer, but of everyone that is truly awakened? But what have I wrote, to this day, which is either stronger or plainer?

8

The Full Assurance of Faith

In August following, I had a long conversation with Arvid Gradin, in Germany. After he had given me an account of his experience, I desired him to give me, in writing, a definition of "the full assurance of faith," which he did in the following words: —

Requies in sanguine Christi; firma fiducia in Deum, et persuasio de gratis Divina; tranquillitas mentis summa, atque serenitas et pax; cum absentia omnis desiderii carnalis, et cessatione peccatorum etiam internorum.

"Repose in the blood of Christ; a firm confidence in God, and persuasion of His favor; the highest tranquility, serenity, and peace of mind, with a deliverance from every fleshly desire, and a cessation of all, even inward sins."

This was the first account I ever heard from any living man, of what I had before learned myself from the oracles of God, and had been praying for (with the little company of my friends), and expecting, for several years.

9

"My Sole Business Be Thy Praise"

In 1739, my brother and I published a volume of *Hymns and Sacred Poems*. In many of these we declared our sentiments strongly and explicitly. So, page 24,—

> Turn the full stream of nature's tide;
>   Let all our actions tend
> To Thee, their source; Thy love the guide,
>   Thy glory be the end.
>
> Earth then a scale to heaven shall be;
>   Sense shall point out the road;
> The creatures all shall lead to Thee,
>   And all we taste be God.

Again,—

> Lord, arm me with Thy Spirit's might,
>   Since I am call'd by Thy great name
> In thee my wand'ring thoughts unite,
>   Of all my works be Thou the aim;
> Thy love attend me all my days
> And my sole business be Thy praise.
>   (Page 122)

Again,—

> Eager for Thee I ask and pant,
>   So strong the principle Divine,
> Carries me out with sweet constraint,
>   Till all my hallow'd soul be Thine;
> Plunged in the Godhead's deepest sea,
> And lost in Thine immensity!
>   (Page 125)

Once more,—

> *Heavenly Adam, life Divine,*
> *Change my nature into Thine;*
> *Move and spread throughout my soul,*
> *Actuate and fill the whole.*

(Page 153)

It would be easy to cite many more passages to the same effect. But these are sufficient to show, beyond contradiction, what our sentiments then were.

10

The Character of a Methodist

Loves God with all his heart, soul,
    mind, and strength
In everything gives thanks
Heart lifted to God at all times
Loves every man as his own soul
Pure in heart
God reigns alone
Keeps *all* the commandments
Does all to the glory of God
Adorns the doctrine of God in all things

The first tract I ever wrote expressly on this subject was published in the latter end of this year. That none might be prejudiced before they read it, I gave it the indifferent title of "The Character of a Methodist." In this I described a perfect Christian, placing in the front, "Not as though I had already attained." Part of it I subjoin without any alteration:—

17

"A Methodist is one who loves the Lord his God with all his heart, with all his soul, with all his mind, and with all his strength. God is the joy of his heart, and the desire of his soul, which is continually crying, 'Whom have I in heaven but Thee? and there is none upon earth whom I desire besides Thee.' My God and my all! 'Thou art the strength of my heart, and my portion forever.' He is therefore happy in God; yea, always happy, as having in him a well of water springing up into everlasting life, and overflowing his soul with peace and joy. Perfect love having now cast out fear, he rejoices evermore. Yea, his joy is full, and all his bones cry out, 'Blessed be the God and Father of our Lord Jesus Christ, who, according to His abundant mercy, hath begotten me again unto a living hope of an inheritance incorruptible and undefiled, reserved in heaven for me.'

"And he who hath this hope, thus full of immortality, in every thing giveth thanks, as knowing this (whatsoever it is) is the will of God in Christ Jesus concerning him. From Him, therefore, he cheerfully receives all, saying, 'Good is the will of the Lord;' and whether He giveth or taketh away, equally blessing the name of the Lord. Whether in ease or pain, whether in sickness or health, whether in life or death, he giveth thanks from the ground of the heart to Him who orders it for good; into whose hands he hath wholly committed his body and soul, 'as into the hands of a faithful Creator.' He is, therefore, anxiously 'careful for nothing,' as having 'cast all his care on Him that careth for him;' and 'in all things' resting on Him after 'making' his 'request known to Him with thanksgiving.'

"For, indeed, he 'prays without ceasing;' at all times the language of his heart is this, 'Unto Thee is my mouth, though without a voice; and my silence speaketh unto Thee.' His heart is lifted up to God at all times, and in all places. In this he is never hindered, much less interrupted, by any person or thing. In retirement or company, in leisure, business, or conversation, his heart is ever with the Lord. Whether he lie down, or rise up, 'God is in all his thoughts:' he walks with God continually; having the loving eye of his soul fixed on Him, and everywhere 'seeing Him that is invisible.'

"And loving God, he 'loves his neighbor as himself;' he loves every man as his own soul. He loves his enemies, yea, and the enemies of God. And if it be not in his power to 'do good to them that hate' him, yet he ceases not to 'pray for them,' though they spurn his love, and still 'despitefully use him, and persecute him.'

"For he is 'pure in heart.' Love has purified his heart from envy, malice, wrath, and every unkind temper. It has cleansed him from pride, whereof 'only cometh contention;' and he hath now 'put on bowels of mercies, kindness, humbleness of mind, meekness, long-suffering.' And, indeed, all possible ground for contention, on his part, is cut off. For none can take from him what he desires, seeing he 'loves not the world, nor any of the things of the world;' but 'all his desire is unto God, and to the remembrance of His name.'

"Agreeable to this his one desire, is the one design of his life; namely, 'to do not his own will, but the will of Him that sent him.' His one intention at all times and in all places is, not to please himself, but Him whom his soul loveth. He hath a single eye; and because his 'eye is single, his whole body is full of light. The whole is light, as when the bright shining of a candle doth enlighten the house.' God reigns alone; all that is in the soul is 'holiness to the Lord.' There is not a motion in his heart but is according to His will. Every thought that arises points to Him, and is in 'obedience to the law of Christ.'

"And the tree is known by its fruits. For, as he loves God, so he 'keeps His commandments;' not only some, or most of them, but all, from the least to the greatest. He is not content to 'keep the whole law and offend in one point,' but has in all points 'a conscience void of offense toward God and toward man.' Whatever God has forbidden, he avoids; whatever God has enjoined, he does. 'He runs the way of God's commandments,' now He hath set his heart at liberty. It is his glory and joy so to do; it is his daily crown of rejoicing, to 'do the will of God on earth, as it is done in heaven.'

"All the commandments of God he accordingly keeps, and that with all his might; for his obedience is in proportion to his love, the source from whence it flows. And therefore, loving God with all his heart, he serves Him with all his strength; he continually presents his soul and 'body a living sacrifice, holy, acceptable to God;' entirely and without reserve devoting himself, all he has, all he is, to His glory. All the talents he has, he constantly employs according to his Master's will; every power and faculty of his soul, every member of his body.

"By consequence, 'whatsoever he doeth, it is all to the glory of God.' In all his employments of every kind, he not only aims at this, which is implied in having a single eye, but actually attains it; his business and his refreshments, as well as his prayers, all serve to this great end. Whether he 'sit in the house, or walk by the way,' whether he lie down, or rise up, he is promoting, in all he speaks or does, the one business of his life. Whether he put on his apparel, or labor, or eat and drink, or divert himself from too wasting labor, it all tends to advance the glory of God, by peace and good will among men. His one invariable rule is this: 'Whatsoever ye do, in word or deed, do it all in the name of the Lord Jesus, giving thanks to God, even the Father through Him.'

"Nor do the customs of the world at all hinder his 'running the race which is set before him.' He cannot, therefore, 'lay up treasures upon earth,' no more than he can take fire into his bosom. He cannot speak evil of his neighbor, any more than he can lie either for God or man. He cannot utter an unkind word of anyone; for love keeps the door of his lips. He cannot 'speak idle words; no corrupt conversation' ever 'comes out of his mouth;' as is all that is not 'good to the use of edifying,' not fit to 'minister grace to the hearers.' But 'whatsoever things are pure, whatsoever things are lovely, whatsoever things are' justly 'of good report,' he thinks, speaks, and acts, 'adorning the doctrine of God our Saviour in all things.' "

These are the very words wherein I largely declared, for the first time, my sentiments of Christian perfection. And, is it not easy to see, (1) That this is the very point at which I aimed all along from the year 1725; and more determinately from the year 1730, when I began to be *homo unius libri,* "a man of one book," regarding none, comparatively, but the Bible? Is it not easy to see, (2) That this is the very same doctrine which I believe and teach at this day; not adding one point, either to that inward or outward holiness which I maintained eight and thirty years ago? And it is the same which, by the grace of God, I have continued to teach from that time till now; as will appear to every impartial person from the extracts subjoined below.

11

The Opposition of Religious Leaders

I do not know that any writer has made any objection against that tract to this day; and for some time, I did not find much opposition upon the head, at least, not from serious persons. But after a time, a cry arose, and, what a little surprised me, among religious men, who affirmed, not that I stated perfection wrong, but that, "there is no perfection on earth;" nay, and fell vehemently on my brother and me for affirming the contrary. We scarce expected so rough an attack from these; especially as we were clear on justification by faith, and careful to ascribe the whole salvation to the mere grace of God. But what most surprised us, was, that we were said to "dishonor Christ," by asserting that He "saveth to the uttermost;" by maintaining He will reign in our hearts alone, and subdue all things to Himself.

12

Views on Christian Perfection

In what sense Christians are not perfect
In what sense they are
A present cleansing

I think it was in the latter end of the year 1740, that I had a conversation with Dr. Gibson, then bishop of London, at Whitehall. He asked me what I meant by perfection. I told him without any disguise or reserve.

When I ceased speaking, he said, "Mr. Wesley, if this be all you mean, publish it to all the world. If anyone then can confute what you say, he may have free leave." I answered, "My Lord, I will;" and accordingly wrote and published, the sermon on Christian perfection.

In this I endeavored to show, (1) In what sense Christians are not, (2) In what sense they are, perfect.

" (1) *In what sense they are not.* They are not perfect in knowledge. They are not free from ignorance, no, nor from mistake. We are no more to expect any living man to be infallible, than to be omniscient. They are not free from infirmities, such as weakness or slowness of understanding, irregular quickness or heaviness of imagination. Such in another kind are impropriety of language, ungracefulness of pronunciation; to which one might add a thousand nameless defects, either in conversation or behavior. From such infirmities as these none are perfectly freed till their spirits return to God; neither can we expect till then to be wholly freed from temptation; for 'the servant is not above his master.' But neither in this sense is there any absolute perfection on earth. There is no perfection of degrees, none which does not admit of a continual increase.

" (2) *In what sense then are they perfect?* Observe, we are not now speaking of babes in Christ, but adult Christians. But even babes in Christ are so far perfect as not to commit sin. This St. John affirms expressly; and it cannot be disproved by the examples of the Old Testament. For what if the holiest of the ancient Jews did sometimes commit sin? We cannot infer from hence, that, 'all Christians do and must commit sin as long as they live.'

"But does not the Scriptures say, 'A just man sinneth seven times a day?' It does not. Indeed, it says, 'A just man falleth seven times.' But this is quite another thing; for, First, the words, *a day*, are not in the text.

Secondly, here is no mention of *falling into sin* at all. What is here mentioned, is *falling into temporal affliction.*

"But elsewhere Solomon says, 'There is no man that sinneth not.' Doubtless thus it was in the days of Solomon; yea, and from Solomon to Christ there was then no man that sinned not. But whatever was the case of those under the law, we may safely affirm, with St. John, that, since the Gospel was given 'he that is born of God sinneth not.'

"The privileges of Christians are in no wise to be measured by what the Old Testament records concerning those who were under the Jewish dispensation; seeing the fulness of time is now come, the Holy Ghost is now given, the great salvation of God is now brought to men by the revelation of Jesus Christ. The kingdom of heaven is now set upon earth, concerning which the Spirit of God declared of old time (so far is David from being the pattern or standard of Christian perfection), 'He that is feeble among them, at that day, shall be as David, and the house of David shall be as the angel of the Lord before them,' Zech. xii. 8.

"But the Apostles themselves committed sin; Peter by dissembling, Paul by his sharp contention with Barnabas. Suppose they did, will you argue this: 'If two of the Apostles once committed sin, then all other Christians in all ages, do and must commit sin as long as they live?' Nay, God forbid we should thus speak. No necessity of sin was laid upon them; the grace of God was surely sufficient for them. And it is sufficient for us at this day.

"But St. James says, 'In many things we offend all.' True: but who are the persons here spoken of? Why, those many masters or teachers whom God had not sent; not the apostle himself, nor any real Christian. That in the word we, used by a figure of speech, common in all other as well as the inspired writings, the apostle could not possibly include himself, or any other true believer, appears, First, from the ninth verse, 'Therewith bless we God, and therewith curse we men.' Surely not we apostles! not we believers! Secondly, from the words preceding the text: 'My brethren, be not many masters,' or teachers, 'knowing that we shall receive the greater condemnation. For in many things we offend all.' We! Who? Not the apostles nor true believers, but they who were to 'receive the greater condemnation,' because of those many offenses. Nay, Thirdly, the verse itself proves, that, 'we offend all,' cannot be spoken either of all men or all Christians. For in it immediately follows the mention of a man who "offends not,' as the *we* first mentioned did; from whom therefore he is professedly contradistinguished, and pronounced a 'perfect man.'

"But St. John himself says, 'If we say we have no sin, we deceive ourselves;' and, 'If we say we have not sinned, we make Him a liar, and His word is not in us.'

"I answer, (1) The tenth verse fixes the sense of the eighth: 'If we say we have no sin,' in the former, being explained by, 'If we say we have not sinned,' in the latter verse. (2) The point under consideration is not whether we have not sinned, heretofore; and neither of these verses asserts that we do sin, or commit sin now. (3) The ninth verse explains both the eighth and tenth: 'If we confess our sins, he is faithful and just to forgive us our sins, and to cleanse us from all unrighteousness.' As if He had said, 'I have before affirmed, The blood of Christ cleanseth from all sin.' And no man can say, 'I need it not; I have no sin to be cleansed from.' 'If we say, we have no sin,' that, 'we have not sinned, we deceive ourselves,' and make God a liar: but, 'if we confess our sins,' but also 'to cleanse us from all unrighteousness,' that we may 'go and sin no more.' In conformity, therefore, both to the doctrine of St. John, and the whole tenor of the New Testament, we fix this conclusion: A Christian is so far perfect, as not to commit sin.

"This is the glorious privilege of every Christian, yea, though he be but a babe in Christ. But it is only of grown Christians it can be affirmed, they are in such a sense perfect, as, Secondly, to be freed from evil thoughts and evil tempers. First from evil or sinful thoughts. Indeed, whence should they spring? 'Out of the heart of man,' if at all, 'proceed evil thoughts.' If, therefore, the heart be no longer evil, then evil thoughts no longer proceed out of it: for 'a good tree cannot bring forth evil fruit.'

"And as they are freed from evil thoughts, so likewise from evil tempers. Everyone of these can say, with St. Paul, 'I am crucified with Christ; nevertheless I live; yet not I, but Christ liveth in me;'—words that manifestly describe a deliverance from inward as well as from outward sin. This is expressed both negatively, 'I live not,' my evil nature, the body of sin is destroyed; and positively, 'Christ liveth in me,' and, therefore, all that is holy, and just, and good. Indeed, both these, 'Christ liveth in me,' and 'I live not,' are inseparably connected. For what communion hath light with darkness, or Christ with Belial?

"He therefore, who liveth in these Christians hath 'purified their hearts by faith;' insomuch that everyone that has Christ in him, 'the hope of glory, purifieth himself even as He is pure.' He is purified from pride; for Christ was lowly in heart; he is pure from desire and self-will; for Christ desired only to do the will of the Father: and he is pure from anger, in the common sense of the word, for Christ was meek and gentle. I say, *in the common sense of the word;* for He is angry at sin, while He is grieved for the sinner. He feels a displacency at every offense against God, but only tender compassion to the offender.

"Thus doth Jesus save His people from their sins; not only from outward sins, but from the sins of their hearts. 'True,' say some, 'but not till death, not in this world.' Nay, St. John says, 'Herein is our love made perfect, that we may have boldness in the day of judgment; because, as He is, so are we in this world.' The apostle here, beyond all contradiction, speaks of himself and other living Christians, of whom he flatly affirms, that not only at or after death, but 'in this world,' they are 'as their Master.'

"Exactly agreeable to this are his words in the first chapter: 'God is light, and in Him is no darkness at all. If we walk in the light, as He is in the light, we have fellowship one with another, and the blood of Jesus Christ His Son cleanseth us from all sin.' And again: 'If we confess our sins, He is faithful and just to forgive us our sins, and to cleanse us from all unrighteousness.' Now, it is evident the Apostle here speaks of a deliverance wrought in this world: for he saith not, The blood of Christ *will* cleanse (at the hour of death, or in the day of judgment), but it 'cleanseth,' at the time present, us living Christians 'from all sin.' And it is equally evident, that if any sin remain, we are not cleansed from all sin. If any unrighteousness remain in the soul, it is not cleansed from all unrighteousness. Neither let any say that this relates to justification only, or the cleansing us from the guilt of sin: first, because this is confounding together what the Apostle clearly distinguishes, who mentions, first, 'to forgive us our sins,' and then 'to cleanse us from all unrighteousness.' Secondly, because this is asserting justification by works, in the strongest sense possible; it is making all inward, as well as all outward, holiness, necessarily previous to justification. For if the cleansing here spoken of is no other than the cleansing us from the guilt of sin, then we are not cleansed from guilt, that is, not justified, unless on condition of walking 'in the light, as He is in the light.' It remains, then, that Christians are saved in this world from all sin, from all unrighteousness; that they are now in such a sense perfect, as not to commit sin, and to be freed from evil thoughts and evil tempers."

It could not be, but that a discourse of this kind, which directly contradicted the favorite opinion of many, who were esteemed by others, and possibly esteemed themselves, some of the best of Christians (whereas, if these things were so, they were not Christians at all), should give no small offense. Many answers or animadversions, therefore, were expected; but I was agreeably disappointed. I do not know that any appeared; so I went quietly on my way.

13

Two Works of Grace

Qualities of cleansed hearts
When a person becomes a child of God
Remission and cleansing not received
    concurrently

Not long after, I think in the spring, 1741, we published a second volume of hymns. As the doctrine was still misunderstood, and conseqently misrepresented, I judged it needful to explain yet farther upon the head; which was done in the preface to it as follows: —

"This great gift of God, the salvation of our souls, is no other than the image of God fresh stamped on our hearts. It is a 'renewal of believers in the spirit of their minds, after the likeness of Him that created them.' God hath now laid 'the axe unto the root of the tree, purifying their hearts by faith,' and 'cleansing all the thoughts of their hearts by the inspiration of His Holy Spirit.' Having this hope, that they shall see God as He is, they 'purify themselves even as He is pure,' and are 'holy, as He that hath called them is holy, in all manner of conversation.' Not that they have already attained all that they shall attain, either are already in this sense perfect. But they daily 'go on from strength to strength, beholding' now, 'as in a glass, the glory of the Lord, they are changed into the same image, from glory to glory, by the Spirit of the Lord.'

"And 'where the Spirit of the Lord is, there is liberty'; such liberty 'from the law of sin and death,' as the children of this world will not believe, though a man declare it unto them. 'The Son hath made them free, who are thus 'born of God,' from that great root of sin and bitterness, pride. They feel that all their 'sufficiency is of God,' that it is He alone who 'is in all their thoughts,' and 'worketh in them both to will and to do of His good pleasure.' They feel that 'it is not they' that 'speak, but the Spirit of' their 'Father who speaketh' in them, and that whatsoever is done by their hands, 'the Father who is in them, He doeth the works.' So that God is to them all in all, and they are nothing in His sight. They are freed from self-will, as desiring nothing but the holy and perfect will of God: not supplies in want, not ease in pain,[1] nor life, or death, or any creature; but continually crying in their inmost soul, 'Father, Thy will be done.' They are freed from evil thoughts, so that they cannot enter into them, no, not for a moment. Aforetime, when an evil thought came in, they looked up, and it vanished away. But now it does not come in, there being no room for this, in a soul which is full of God. They are free from wanderings in prayer. Whensoever they pour out their hearts in a more immediate manner before God, they have no thought of anything past,[2] or absent, or to come, but of

[1]This is too strong. Our Lord Himself desired ease in pain. He asked for it only with resignation: "Not as I will," I desire, "But as Thou wilt."

[2]This is far too strong. See the sermon "On Wandering Thoughts."

God alone. In times past, they had wandering thoughts darting in, which yet fled away like smoke; but now that smoke does not rise at all. They have no fear or doubt, either as to their state in general, or as to any particular action.[3] The 'unction from the Holy one' teacheth them every hour what they shall do, and what they shall speak;[4] nor, therefore, have they any need to reason concerning it.[5] They are in one sense freed from temptations; for though numberless temptations fly about them, yet they trouble them not.[6] At all times their souls are even and calm, their hearts are steadfast and unmovable. Their peace, flowing as a river, 'passeth all understanding,' and they 'rejoice with joy unspeakable and full of glory.' For they 'are sealed by the Spirit unto the day of redemption,' having the witness in themselves, that there is laid up for them a 'crown of righteousness, which the Lord will give' them 'in that day.'[7]

"Not that every one is a child of the devil, till he is thus renewed in love: on the contrary, whoever has 'a sure confidence in God, that, through the merits of Christ, his sins are forgiven,' he is a child of God, and, if he abide in Him, an heir of all the promises. Neither ought he in any wise to cast away his confidence, or to deny the faith he has received, because it is weak, or because it is 'tried with fire,' so that his soul is 'in heaviness through manifold temptations.'

"Neither dare we affirm, as some have done, that all this salvation is given at once. There is, indeed, an instantaneous, as well as a gradual work of God in His

[3]Frequently this is the case; but only for a time.

[4]For a time it may be so; but not always.

[5]Sometimes they have no need; at other times they have.

[6]Sometimes they do not; at other times they do, and that grievously.

[7]Not all who are saved from sin; many of them have not attained it yet.

children; and there wants not, we know, a cloud of witnesses, who have received, in one moment, either a clear sense of the forgiveness of their sins, or the abiding witness of the Holy Spirit. But we do not know a single instance, in any place, of a person's receiving, in one and the same moment, remission of sins, the abiding witness of the Spirit, and a new, a clean heart.

"Indeed, how God may work, we cannot tell; but the general manner wherein He does work, is this: those who once trusted in themselves that they were righteous, that they were rich, and increased in goods, and had need of nothing, are, by the Spirit of God applying His word, convinced that they are poor and naked. All the things that they have done are brought to their remembrance and set in array before them, so that they see the wrath of God hanging over their heads, and feel that they deserve the damnation of hell. In their trouble they cry unto the Lord, and He shows them that He hath taken away their sins, and opens the kingdom of Heaven in their hearts,—'righteousness, and peace, and joy in the Holy Ghost.' Sorrow and pain are fled away, and 'sin has no more dominion over' them. Knowing they are justified freely through faith in His blood, they 'have peace with God through Jesus Christ'; they 'rejoice in hope of the glory of God,' and 'the love of God is shed abroad in their hearts.'

"In this peace they remain for days, or weeks, or months, and commonly suppose they shall not know war any more; till some of their old enemies, their bosom sins, or the sin which did most easily beset them (perhaps anger or desire), assault them again, and thrust sore at them, that they may fall. Then arises fear that they shall not endure to the end; and often doubt whether God has not forgotten them, or whether they did not deceive themselves in thinking their sins were forgiven. Under these clouds, especially if they reason with the devil, they go mourning all the day long. But it is seldom long before their Lord answers for Himself, sending them the Holy Ghost to comfort them, to bear witness continually with their spirits that they are the children of God. Then they are, indeed, meek, and gentle, and teachable, even as a little child.

"And now first do they see the ground of their heart,[8] which God before would not disclose unto them, lest the soul should fail before Him, and the spirit which He had made. Now they see all the hidden abominations there, the depths of pride, self-will, and hell; yet having the witness in themselves, 'Thou art an heir of God, a joint heir with Christ, even in the midst of this fiery trial;' which continually heightens both the strong sense they then have of their inability to help themselves, and the inexpressible hunger they feel after a full renewal in His image, in 'righteousness and true holiness.'

"Then God is mindful of the desire of them that fear Him, and gives them a single eye, and a pure heart; He stamps upon them His own image and super-scription; He createth them anew in Christ Jesus; He cometh unto them with His Son and blessed Spirit, and, fixing His abode in their souls, bringeth them into the 'rest which remaineth for the people of God.' "

Here I cannot but remark, (1) That this is the strongest account we ever gave of Christian perfection,— indeed, too strong in more than one particular, as is observed in the notes annexed. (2) That there is nothing which we have since advanced upon the subject, either in verse or prose, which is not either directly or indirectly contained in this preface. So that whether our present doctrine be right or wrong, it is, however, the same which we taught from the beginning.

[8]Is it not astonishing, that while this book is extant, which was published four and twenty years ago, any one should face me down, that this is new doctrine, and what I never taught before?

14

The Rest That Remains

A high experience
Receivable by mere faith
Instantaneous
Attainable now

I need not give additional proofs of this, by multiplying quotations from the volume itself. It may suffice to cite part of one hymn only, the last in that volume: —

> Lord, I believe a rest remains,
>   To all Thy people known;
> A rest where pure enjoyment reigns,
>   And thou art loved alone;
>
> A rest where all our soul's desire
>   Is fixed on things above;
> Where doubt and pain and fear expire,
>   Cast out by perfect love.
>
> From every evil motion freed,
>   (The Son hath made us free,)
> On all the powers of hell we tread,
>   In glorious liberty.
>
> Safe in the way of life, above
>   Death, earth, and hell we rise;
> We find, when perfected in love,
>   Our long-sought paradise.
>
> Oh, that I now the rest might know,
>   Believe and enter in!
> Now, Saviour, now the power bestow,
>   And let me cease from sin!

Remove this hardness from my heart,
  This unbelief remove;
To me the rest of faith impart,
  The sabbath of Thy love.

Come, O my Saviour, come away!
  Into my soul descend!
No longer from Thy creature stay,
  My author and my end.

The bliss Thou hast for me prepared,
  No longer be delayed;
Come, my exceeding great reward,
  For whom I first was made.

Come Father, Son, and Holy Ghost,
  And seal me Thine abode!
Let all I am in Thee be lost;
  Let all be lost in God!

Can anything be more clear than, (1) That here, also, is as full and high a salvation as we have ever spoken of? (2) That this is spoken of as receivable by mere faith, and as hindered only by unbelief? (3) That this faith, and consequently the salvation which it brings, is spoken of as given in an instant? (4) That it is supposed that instant may be now? that we need not stay another moment? that "now," the very "now is the accepted time? now is the day of" this full "salvation?" And, lastly, that, if any speak otherwise, he is the person that brings new doctrine among us?

15

Misunderstandings Concerning Perfection

No dispensation from religious exercises
No deliverance from human mistakes
Sanctified throughout—in body, soul,
    and spirit
Dominated by love to God and man
Showing forth God's praise in word,
    thought, and deed.

About a year after, namely, in the year 1742, we published another volume of hymns. The dispute being now at the height, we spoke upon the head more largely than ever before. Accordingly, abundance of the hymns in this volume treat expressly on this subject. And so does the preface, which, as it is short, it may not be amiss to insert entire: —

"(1) Perhaps the general prejudice against Christian perfection may chiefly arise from a misapprehension of the nature of it. We willingly allow and continually declare, there is no such perfection in this life, as implies either a dispensation from doing good, and attending all the ordinances of God, or a freedom from ignorance, mistake, temptation, and a thousand infirmities necessarily connected with flesh and blood.

"(2) First. We not only allow, but earnestly contend, that there is no perfection in this life, which implies any dispensation from attending all the ordinances of God, or from doing good unto all men while we have time, though 'especially unto the household of faith.' We believe, that not only the babes in Christ, who have newly found redemption in His blood, but those also who are 'grown up into perfect men,' are indispensably obliged, as often as they have opportunity, 'to eat bread and drink wine in remembrance of Him,' and to 'search the Scriptures;' by fasting, as well as temperance, to 'keep their bodies under, and bring them into subjection;' and, above all, to pour out their souls in prayer, both secretly, and in the great congregation.

" (3) We secondly believe that there is no such perfection in this life, as implies an entire deliverance, either from ignorance, or mistake, in things not essential to salvation, or from manifold temptations, or from numberless infirmities, wherewith the corrupible body more or less presses down the soul. We cannot find any ground in Scripture to suppose, that any inhabitant of a house of clay is wholly exempt either from bodily infirmities, or from ignorance of many things; or to imagine any is incapable of mistake, or falling into divers temptations.

" (4) But whom, then, do you mean by 'one that is perfect'? We mean one in whom is 'the mind which was in Christ,' and who so 'walketh as Christ also walked'; a man 'that hath clean hands and a pure heart,' or that is 'cleansed from all filthiness of flesh and spirit'; one in whom is 'no occasion of stumbling,' and who, accordingly, 'does not commit sin.' To declare this a little more particularly: we understand by that Scriptural expression, 'a perfect man,' one in whom God hath fulfilled His faithful word, 'From all your filthiness and from all your idols I will cleanse you: I will also save you from all your uncleannesses.' We understand, hereby, one whom God hath 'sanctified throughout in body, soul, and spirit'; one who 'walketh in the light as He is in the light, in whom is no darkness at all; the blood of Jesus Christ His Son having cleansed him from all sin.'

"(5) This man can now testify to all mankind, 'I am crucified with Christ: nevertheless I live; yet not I, but Christ liveth in me.' He is 'holy as God who called' him 'is holy,' both in heart and 'in all manner of conversation.' He 'loveth the Lord his God with all his heart,' and serveth him 'with all his strength.' He 'loveth his neighbor,' every man, 'as himself'; yea, 'as Christ loveth us'; them, in particular, that 'despitefully use him and persecute him, because they know not the Son, neither the Father.' Indeed, his soul is all love, filled with 'bowels of mercies, kindness, meekness, gentleness, long-suffering.' And his life agreeth thereto, full of 'the work of faith, the patience of hope, the labor of love.' 'And whatsoever' he 'doeth either in word or deed,' he 'doeth it all in the name,' in the love and power, 'of the Lord Jesus.' In a word, he doeth 'the will of God on earth, as it is done in heaven.'

"(6) This it is to be a perfect man, to be 'sanctified throughout;' even 'to have a heart so all-flaming with the love of God' (to use Archbishop Ussher's words), 'as continually to offer up every thought, word, and work, as a spiritual sacrifice, acceptable to God through Christ.' In every thought of our hearts, in every word of our tongues, in every work of our hands, to 'show forth His praise, who hath called us out of darkness into His marvellous light.' O that both we, and all who seek the Lord Jesus in sincerity, may thus 'be made perfect in one!'"

This is the doctrine which we preached from the beginning, and which we preach at this day. Indeed, by viewing it in every point of light, and comparing it again and again with the word of God on the one hand, and the experience of the children of God on the other, we saw farther into the nature and properties of Christian perfection. But still there is no contrariety at all between our first and our last sentiments. Our first conception of it was, It is to have "the mind which was in Christ," and to "walk as He walked"; to have all the mind that was in Him, and always to walk as He walked: in other words, to be inwardly and outwardly devoted to God; all devoted in heart and life. And we have the same conception of it now, without either addition or diminution.

16

Holiness Hymns

The hymns concerning it in this volume are too numerous to transcribe. I shall only cite a part of three: —

> *Saviour from sin, I wait to prove*
> * That Jesus is Thy healing name;*
> *To lose when perfected in love,*
> * Whate'er I have, or can, or am;*
> *I stay me on Thy faithful word,*
> *"The servant shall be as his Lord."*
>
> *Answer that gracious end in me*
> * For which Thy precious life was given;*
> *Redeem from all iniquity,*
> * Restore, and make me meet for heaven.*
> *Unless Thou purge my every stain,*
> *Thy suffering and my faith is vain.*
>
> *Didst Thou not die, that I might live,*
> * No longer to myself but Thee?*
> *Might body, soul, and spirit give*
> * To Him who gave himself for me?*
> *Come then, my Master and my God,*
> *Take the dear purchase of Thy blood.*

Thy own peculiar servant claim,
For Thy own truth and mercy's sake;
Hallow in me Thy glorious name;
Me for Thine own this moment take;
And change and throughly purify;
Thine only may I live and die.

(Page 80)

Chose from the world, if now I stand,
Adorn'd with righteousness Divine;
If brought into the promised land,
I justly call the Saviour mine;

The sanctifying Spirit pour,
To quench my thirst and wash me clean,
Now, Saviour, let the gracious shower
Descend, and make me pure from sin.

Purge me from every sinful blot:
My idols all be cast aside:
Cleanse me from every evil thought,
From all the filth of self and pride.

The hatred of the carnal mind
Out of my flesh at once remove:
Give me a tender heart, resign'd,
And pure, and full of faith and love.

Oh that I now, from sin released,
Thy word might to the utmost prove,
Enter into Thy promised rest;
The Canaan of Thy perfect love!

Now let me gain perfection's height!
Now let me into nothing fall;
Be less than nothing in my sight,
And feel that Christ is all in all.

(Page 258)

39

Lord, I believe, Thy work of grace
  Is perfect in the soul:
His heart is pure who sees Thy face,
  His spirit is made whole.

From every sickness, by Thy word,
  From every foul disease,
Saved, and to perfect health restored,
  To perfect holiness:

He walks in glorious liberty,
  To sin entirely dead:
The Truth, the Son hath made him free,
  And he is free indeed.

Throughout his soul Thy glories shine,
  His soul is all renew'd,
And deck'd in righteousness Divine,
  And clothed and fill'd with God.

This is the rest, the life, the peace,
  Which all Thy people prove;
Love is the bond of perfectness,
  And all their soul is love.

O joyful sound of Gospel grace!
  Christ shall in me appear;
I, even I, shall see His face,
  I shall be holy here!

He visits now the house of clay,
  He shakes his future home;
O wouldst Thou, Lord, on this glad day,
  Into Thy temple come!

Come, O my God, Thyself reveal,
  Fill all this mighty void;
Thou only canst my spirit fill:
  Come, O my God, my God!

Fulfil, fulfil my large desires,
  Large as infinity!
Give, give me all my soul requires,
  All, all that is in Thee!

17

Questions and Answers on the Doctrine of Sanctification

What is it?
When is it received?
The support of Scripture
The divine command
Examples of Christian perfection

On Monday, June 25, 1744, our first conference began; six clergymen and all our preachers being present. The next morning we seriously considered the doctrine of sanctification, or perfection. The questions asked concerning it, and the substance of the answers given were as follows: —

"What is it to be sanctified?

"To be renewed in the image of God, "in righteousness and true holiness.'

"What is implied in being a perfect Christian?

"The loving God with all our heart, and mind, and soul (Deut. vi. 5).

"Does this imply, that all inward sin is taken away?

"Undoubtedly; or how can we be said to be 'saved from all our uncleannesses?' (Ezek. xxxvi. 29)."

41

Our second conference began August 1, 1745. The next morning we spoke of sanctification as follows: —

"When does inward sanctification begin?

"In the moment a man is justified. (Yet sin remains in him, yea, the seed of all sin, till he is sanctified throughout). From that time a believer gradually dies to sin, and grows in grace.

"Is this ordinarily given till a little before death?

"It is not, to those who expect it no sooner.

"But may we expect it sooner?

"Why not? For, although we grant, (1) that the generality of believers, whom we have hitherto known, were not so sanctified till near death; (2) that few of those to whom St. Paul wrote his Epistles were so at that time; nor, (3) he himself at the time of writing his former Epistles; yet all this does not prove, that we may not be so today.

"In what manner should we preach sanctification?

"Scarce at all to those who are not pressing forward; to those who are, always by way of promise; always drawing, rather than driving."

Our third conference began Tuesday, May 26, 1746.

In this we carefully read over the minutes of the two preceding conferences, to observe whether anything contained therein might be retrenched or altered on more mature consideration. But we did not see cause to alter in any respect what we had agreed upon before.

Our fourth conference began on Tuesday, June the 16th, 1747. As several persons were present, who did not believe the doctrine of perfection, we agreed to examine it from the foundation.

In order to this, it was asked,

"How much is allowed by our brethren who differ from us with regard to entire sanctification?

"They grant, (1) That every one must be entirely sanctified in the article of death. (2) That till then, a believer daily grows in grace, comes nearer and nearer to perfection. (3) That we ought to be continually pressing after it, and to exhort all others so to do.

"What do we allow them?

"We grant, (1) That many of those who have died in the faith, yea, the greater part of those we have known, were not perfected in love, till a little before their death. (2) That the term *sanctified,* is continually applied by St. Paul, to all that were justified. (3) That by this term alone, he rarely, if ever, means, 'saved from all sin.' (4) That, consequently, it is not proper to use it in that sense, without adding the word *wholly, entirely,* or the like. (5) That the inspired writers almost continually speak of, or to, those who were justified, but very rarely of, or to, those who were wholly sanctified.[9] (6) That, consequently, it behooves us to speak almost continually of the state of justification; but more rarely,[10] 'at least in full and explicit terms, concerning entire sanctification.'

"What, then, is the point where we divide?

"It is this: should we expect to be saved from all sin before the article of death?

"Is there any clear Scripture promise of this,—that God will save us from all sin?

"There is: 'He shall redeem Israel from all his sins,' Psa. cxxx. 8.

"This is more largely expressed in the prophecy of

[9]That is, unto those alone, exclusive of others; but they speak to them jointly with others, almost continually.

[10]More rarely, I allow; but yet in some places, very frequently, strongly, and explicitly.

43

Ezekiel: 'Then will I sprinkle clean water upon you, and ye shall be clean; from all your filthiness, and from all your idols, will I cleanse you; I will also save you from all your uncleannesses,' xxxvi. 25, 29. No promise can be more clear. And to this the Apostle plainly refers in that exhortation: 'Having these promises, let us cleanse ourselves from all filthiness of flesh and spirit, perfecting holiness in the fear of God,' 2 Cor. vii. 1. Equally clear and express is that ancient promise: 'The Lord thy God will circumcise thy heart, and the heart of thy seed, to love the Lord thy God with all thy heart and with all thy soul,' Deut. xxx. 6.

"But does any assertion answerable to this, occur in the New Testament?

"There does, and that laid down in the plainest terms. So 1 John iii. 8: 'For this purpose the Son of God was manifested, that He might destroy the works of the devil;' the works of the devil, without any limitation or restriction; but all sin is the work of the devil. Parallel to which, is the assertion of St. Paul: 'Christ loved the Church, and gave Himself for it, that He might present it to Himself, a glorious Church, not having spot or wrinkle, or any such thing, but that it might be holy and without blemish,' Eph. v. 25-27.

"And to the same effect is his assertion in the eighth of the Romans, verses 3, 4: 'God sent His Son, that the righteousness of the law might be fulfilled in us, who walk not after the flesh, but after the Spirit.'

"Does the New Testament afford any further ground for expecting to be saved from all sin?

"Undoubtedly it does; both in those prayers and commands, which are equivalent to the strongest assertions.

"What prayers do you mean?

"Prayers for entire sanctification; which, were there no such thing, would be mere mockery of God. Such,

44

in particular, are (1) 'Deliver us from evil.' Now, when this is done, when we are delivered from all evil, there can be no sin remaining. (2) 'Neither pray I for these alone, but for them also who shall believe on Me through their word; that they all may be one; as Thou, Father, art in Me, and I in Thee, that they also may be one in us; I in them, and Thou in Me, that they may be made perfect in one,' John xvii. 20-23. (3) 'I bow my knees unto the God and Father of our Lord Jesus Christ, that He would grant you, that ye, being rooted and grounded in love, may be able to comprehend, with all saints, what is the breadth, and length, and depth, and height, and to know the love of Christ, which passeth knowledge; that ye may be filled with all the fulness of God,' Eph. iii. 14, etc. (4) 'The very God of peace sanctify you wholly. And I pray God, your whole spirit, soul, and body, may be preserved blameless unto the coming of our Lord Jesus Christ,' 1 Thess. v. 23.

"What command is there to the same effect?

" (1) 'Be ye perfect, as your Father who is in heaven, is perfect,' Matt. v. 48. (2) 'Thou shalt love the Lord thy God with all thy heart, and with all thy soul, and with all thy mind,' Matt. xxii. 37. But if the love of God fill all the heart, there can be no sin therein.

"But how does it appear that this is to be done before the article of death?

" (1) From the very nature of a command, which is not given to the dead, but to the living. Therefore, 'Thou shalt love God with all thy heart,' cannot mean 'Thou shalt do this when thou diest,' but, while thou livest.

" (2) From express texts of Scripture: (i) 'The grace of God, that bringeth salvation, hath appeared to all men; teaching us that, having renounced ungodliness and worldly lusts, we should live soberly, righteously, and godly in this present world; looking for the glorious appearing of our Lord Jesus Christ, who gave Himself for us, that He might redeem us from all iniquity, and purify unto Himself a peculiar people, zealous of good works,' Titus ii. 11-14; (ii) 'He hath raised up a horn of salvation for us, to perform the mercy promised to our fathers; the oath which He sware to our father Abraham, that He would grant unto us, that we, being delivered out of the hands of our enemies, should serve Him without fear, in holiness and righteousness before Him, all the days of our life,' Luke i. 69, etc.

"Is there any example in Scripture, of persons who had attained to this?

"Yes; St. John, and all those of whom he says, 'Herein is our love made perfect, that we may have boldness in the day of judgment; because, as He is, so are we in this world,' 1 John iv. 17.

"Can you show one such example now? Where is he that is thus perfect?

"To some that make this inquiry, one might answer, If I knew one here, I would not tell you; for you do not enquire out of love. You are like Herod; you only seek the young child to slay it.

"But more directly we answer: There are many reasons why there should be few, if any, indisputable examples. What inconveniences would this bring on the person himself, set as a mark for all to shoot at! And how unprofitable would it be to gainsayers! 'For if they hear not Moses and the Prophets,' Christ and His Apostles, 'neither would they be persuaded though one rose from the dead.'

"Are we not apt to have a secret distaste to any who say they are saved from all sin?

"It is very possible we may, and that upon several grounds; partly from a concern for the good of souls, who may be hurt if these are not what they profess; partly from a kind of implicit envy at those who speak of higher attainments than our own; and partly from our natural slowness and unreadiness of heart to believe the works of God.

"*Why may we not continue in the joy of faith, till we are perfected in love?*

"Why indeed? since holy grief does not quench this joy; since even while we are under the cross, while we deeply partake of the sufferings of Christ, we may rejoice with joy unspeakable."

From these extracts, it undeniably appears, not only what was mine and my brother's judgment, but what was the judgment of all the preachers in connection with us, in the years 1744, 45, 46, and 47. Nor do I remember that, in any one of these conferences, we had one dissenting voice; but whatever doubts any one had when we met, they were all removed before we parted.

18

"Hymns and Sacred Poems"

Deliverance from all sin
Received merely by faith
Given instantaneously
To be expected at any moment

In the year 1749, my brother printed two volumes of "Hymns and Sacred Poems." As I did not see these before they were published, there were some things in them which I did not approve of. But I quite approved of the main of the hymns of this head; a few verses of which are subjoined;—

> *Come, Lord, be manifested here,*
> *And all the devil's works destroy;*

Now, without sin, in me appear,
And fill with everlasting joy;
Thy beatific face display;
Thy presence is the perfect day.
(Vol. I, p. 203)

Swift to my rescue come,
Thy own this moment seize;
Gather my wandring spirit home,
And keep in perfect peace.

Suffer'd no more to rove
O'er all the earth abroad,
Arrest the pris'ner of Thy love,
And shut me up in God!
(Page 247)

Thy pris'ners release, vouchsafe us Thy peace;
And our sorrows and sins in a moment shall cease.
That moment be now! Our petition allow,
Our present Redeemer and Comforter Thou!
(Vol. II, p. 124)

From this inbred sin deliver;
Let the yoke now be broke;
Make me Thine forever.

Partner of Thy perfect nature,
Let me be now in Thee
A new, sinless creature.
(Page 156)

Turn me, Lord, and turn me now,
To Thy yoke my spirit bow;
Grant me now the pearl to find
Of a meek and quiet mind.

Calm, O calm my troubled breast;
Let me gain that second rest;
From my works for ever cease,
Perfected in holiness.
(Page 168)

48

Come in this accepted hour,
  Bring Thy heavenly kingdom in!
Fill us with the glorious power,
  Rooting out the seeds of sin.

(Page 162)

Come, Thou dear Lamb, for sinners slain,
  Bring in the cleansing flood:
Apply, to wash out every stain,
  Thine efficacious blood.

O let it sink into our soul
  Deep as the inbred sin;
Make every wounded spirit whole,
  And every leper clean!

(Page 171)

Pris'ners of hope, arise,
  And see your Lord appear;
Lo! on wings of love he flies,
  And brings redemption near.

Redemption in His blood
  He calls you to receive;
"Come unto Me, the pard'ning God;
  Believe," He cries, "believe!"

Jesus, to Thee we look,
  Till saved from sin's remains,
Reject the inbred tyrant's yoke,
  And cast away his chains.

Our nature shall no more
  O'er us dominion have;
By faith we apprehend the power,
  Which shall for ever save.

(Page 188)

Jesus, our life, in us appear,
Who daily die Thy death;
Reveal Thyelf the finisher;
Thy quick'ning Spirit breathe!

Unfold the hidden mystery,
The second gift impart;
Reveal Thy glorious self in me,
In every waiting heart.

(Page 195)

In Him we have peace, in Him we have power!
Preserved by His grace Throughout the dark hour
In all our temptations He keeps us, to prove
His utmost salvation, His fulness of love.

Pronounce the glad word, And bid us be free!
Oh, hast Thou not, Lord, a blessing for me?
The peace Thou hast given, This moment impart,
And open Thy heaven, O Love, in my heart!

(Page 324)

A second edition of these hymns was published in the year 1752; and that without any other alteration, than that of a few literal mistakes.

I have been the more large in these extracts, because, hence, it appears, beyond all possibility of exception, that to this day, both my brother and I maintained, (1) That Christian perfection is that love of God and our neighbor, which implies deliverance from all sin. (2) That this is received merely by faith. (3) That it is given instantaneously, in one moment. (4) That we are to expect it, not at death, but every moment; that now is the accepted time, now is the day of this salvation.

19

Thoughts on Christian Perfection

What it includes
What it does not include
General observations

At the conference in the year 1759, perceiving some danger that a diversity of sentiments should insensibly steal in among us, we again largely considered this doctrine; and soon after I published "Thoughts on Christian Perfection," prefaced with the following advertisement: —

"The following tract is by no means designed to gratify the curiosity of any man. It is not intended to prove the doctrine at large, in opposition to those who explode and ridicule it; no, nor to answer the numerous objections against it, which may be raised, even by serious men. All I intend here, is simply to declare what are my sentiments on this head; what Christian perfection does, according to my apprehension, include, and what it does not; and to add a few practical observations and directions relative to the subject.

"As these thoughts were at first thrown together, by way of question and answer, I let them continue in the same form. They are just the same that I have entertained for above twenty years.

"What is Christian perfection?

"The loving God with all our heart, mind, soul, and strength. This implies, that no wrong temper, none contrary to love, remains in the soul; and that all the thoughts, words and actions, are governed by pure love.

"Do you affirm that this perfection excludes all infirmities, ignorance, and mistake?

"I continually affirm quite the contrary, and always have done so.

"But how can every thought, word, and work, be governed, by pure love, and the man be subject, at the same time, to ignorance and mistake?

"I see no contradiction here: 'A man may be filled with pure love, and still be liable to mistake.' Indeed, I do not expect to be freed from actual mistakes, till this mortal puts on immortality. I believe this to be a natural consequence of the soul's dwelling in flesh and blood. For we cannot now think at all, but by the mediation of those bodily organs which have suffered equally with the rest of our frame. And hence we cannot avoid sometimes thinking wrong, till this corrupible shall have put on incorruption.

"But we may carry this thought farther yet. A mistake in judgment may possibly occasion a mistake in practice. For instance: Mr. DeRenty's mistake touching the nature of mortification, arising from prejudice of education, occasioned that practical mistake, his wearing an iron girdle. And a thousand such instances there may be, even in those who are in the highest state of grace. Yet, where every word and action springs from love, such a mistake is not openly a sin. However, it cannot bear the rigor of God's justice, but needs the atoning blood.

"What was the judgment of all our brethren who met at Bristol in August 1758, on this head?

"It was expressed in these words: (1) Every one may mistake as long as he lives. (2) A mistake in opinion may occasion a mistake in practice. (3) Every such mistake is a transgression of the perfect law. Therefore, (4) Every such mistake, were it not for the blood of atonement, would expose to eternal damnation. (5) It follows, that the most perfect have continual need of the merits of Christ, even for their actual transgressions, and may say for themselves, as well as for their brethren, 'Forgive us our trespasses.'

"This easily accounts for what might otherwise seem to be utterly unaccountable; namely, that those who are not offended when we speak of the highest degree of love, yet will not hear of living without sin. The reason is, they know all men are liable to mistake, and that in practice as well as in judgment. But they do not know, or do not observe, that this is not sin, if love is the sole principle of action.

"But still, if they live without sin, does not this exclude the necessity of a Mediator? At least, is it not plain that they stand no longer in need of Christ in His priestly office?

"Far from it. None feel their need of Christ like these; none so entirely depend upon Him. For Christ does not give life to the soul separate from, but in and with, Himself. Hence His words are equally true of all men, in whatsoever state of grace they are: 'As the branch cannot bear fruit of itself, except it abide in the vine; no more can ye, except ye abide in me: without' (or separate from) 'me ye can do nothing.'

"In every state we need Christ in the following respects, (1) Whatever grace we receive, it is a free gift from Him. (2) We receive it as His purchase, merely in consideration of the price He paid. (3) We have this grace, not only from Christ, but in Him. For our perfection is not like that of a tree, which flourishes by the sap derived from its own root, but, as was said before, like that of a branch which, united to the vine, bears fruit; but, severed from it, is dried up and withered. (4) All our blessings, temporal, spiritual, and eternal, depend on His intercession for us, which is one branch of His priestly office, whereof therefore we have always equal need. (5) The best of men still need Christ in His priestly office, to atone for their omissions, their short-comings (as some not improperly speak), their mistakes in judgment and practice, and their defects of various kinds. For these are all deviations from the perfect law, and consequently need an atonement. Yet that they are not properly sins, we apprehend may appear from the words of St. Paul, 'He that loveth, hath fulfilled the law; for love is the fulfilling of the law,' Rom. xiii. 10. Now, mistakes, and whatever infirmities necessarily flow from the corruptible state of the body, are no way contrary to love; nor therefore, in the Scripture sense, sin.

"To explain myself a little farther on this head: (1) Not only sin, properly so called (that is, a voluntary transgression of a known law), but sin, improperly so called (that is, an involuntary transgression of a Divine law, known or unknown), needs atoning blood. (2) I believe there is no such perfection in this life as excludes these involuntary transgressions which I apprehend to be naturally consequent on the ignorance and mistakes inseparable from mortality. (3) Therefore *sinless perfection* is a phrase I never use, lest I should seem to contradict myself. (4) I believe, a person filled with the love of God is still liable to these involuntary transgressions. (5) Such transgressions you may call sins, if you please: I do not, for the reasons above mentioned.

"What advice would you give to those that do, and those that do not, call them so?

"Let those that do not call them sins, never think that themselves or any other persons are in such a state as that they can stand before infinite justice without a Mediator. This must argue either the deepest ignorance, or the highest arrogance and presumption.

"Let those who do call them so, beware how they confound these defects with sins, properly so called.

"But how will they avoid it? How will these be

distinguished from those, if they are all promiscuously called sins? I am much afraid, if we should allow any sins to be consistent with perfection, few would confine the idea to those defects concerning which only the assertion could be true.

"But how can a liableness to mistake consist with perfect love? Is not a person who is perfected in love every moment under its influence? And can any mistake flow from pure love?

"I answer, (1) Many mistakes may consist with pure love; (2) Some may accidentally flow from it: I mean, love itself may incline us to mistake. The pure love of our neighbor, springing from the love of God, thinketh no evil, believeth and hopeth all things. Now, this very temper, unsuspicious, ready to believe and hope the best of all men, may occasion our thinking some men better than they really are. Here then is a manifest mistake, accidentally flowing from pure love.

"How shall we avoid setting perfection too high or too low?

"By keeping to the Bible, and setting it just as high as the Scripture does. It is nothing higher and nothing lower than this,—the pure love of God and man; the loving God with all our heart and soul, and our neighbor as ourselves. It is love governing the heart and life, running though all our tempers, words, and actions.

"Suppose one had attained to this, would you advise him to speak of it?

"At first perhaps he would scarce be able to refrain, the fire would be so hot within him; his desire to declare the loving-kindness of the Lord carrying him away like a torrent. But afterward he might; and then it would be advisable, not to speak of it to them that know not God (it is most likely, it would only provoke them to contradict and blaspheme); nor to others, without some particular reason, without some good in view. And then he should have especial care to avoid all appearance of boasting; to speak with the deepest humility and reverence, giving all the glory to God.

"But would it not be better to be entirely silent, not to speak of it at all?

"By silence, he might avoid many crosses, which will naturally and necessarily ensue, if he simply declare, even among believers, what God has wrought in his soul. If, therefore, such a one were to confer with flesh and blood, he would be entirely silent. But this could not be done with a clear conscience: for undoubtedly he ought to speak. Men do not light a candle to put under a bushel; much less does the all-wise God. He does not raise such a monument of his power and love, to hide it from all mankind. Rather he intends it as a general blessing to those who are simple of heart. He designs thereby, not barely the happiness of that individual person, but the animating and encouraging others to follow after the same blessing. His will is, 'that many shall see it' and rejoice, 'and put their trust in the Lord.' Nor does anything under heaven more quicken the desires of those who are justified, than to converse with those whom they believe to have experienced a still higher salvation. This places that salvation full in their view, and increases their hunger and thirst after it; an advantage which must have been entirely lost, had the person so saved buried himself in silence.

"But is there no way to prevent these crosses which usually fall on those who speak of being thus saved?

"It seems they cannot be prevented altogether, while so much of nature remains even in believers. But something might be done, if the preacher in every place would, (1) Talk freely with all who speak thus; and, (2)

Labor to prevent the unjust or unkind treatment of those in favor of whom there is reasonable proof.

"What is reasonable proof? How may we certainly know one that is saved from all sin?

"We cannot infallibly know one that is thus saved (nor even one that is justified), unless it should please God to endow us with the miraculous discernment of spirits. But we apprehend those would be sufficient proofs to any reasonable man, and such as would leave little room to doubt either the truth or depth of the work: (1) If we had clear evidence of his exemplary behaviour for some time before this supposed change. This would give us reason to believe, he would not 'lie for God,' but speak neither more nor less than he felt; (2) If he gave a distinct account of the time and manner wherein the change was wrought, with sound speech which could not be reproved; and, (3) If it appeared that all his subseqent words and actions were holy and unblamable.

"The short of the matter is this: (1) I have abundant reason to believe this person will not lie; (2) He testifies before God, 'I feel no sin, but all love; I pray, rejoice, and give thanks without ceasing; and I have as clear an inward witness, that I am fully renewed, as that I am justified.' Now, if I have nothing to oppose to this plain testimony, I ought in reason to believe it.

"It avails nothing to object, 'But I know several things wherein he is quite mistaken.' For it has been allowed, that all who are in the body are liable to mistake; and that a mistake in judgment may sometimes occasion a mistake in practice; though great care is to be taken that no ill use be made of this concession. For instance: Even one that is perfected in love may mistake with regard to another person, and may think him, in a particular case, to be more or less faulty than he really is. And hence he may speak to him with more or less severity than the truth requires. And in this sense (though that be not the primary meaning of St. James), 'in many things we offend all.' This, therefore, is no proof at all, that the person so speaking is not perfect.

"But is it not a proof, if he is surprised or fluttered by a noise, a fall, or some sudden danger?

"It is not; for one may start, tremble, change color, or be otherwise disordered in body, while the soul is calmly stayed on God, and remains in perfect peace. Nay, the mind itself may be deeply distressed, may be exceeding sorrowful, may be perplexed and pressed down by heaviness and anguish, even to agony, while the heart cleaves to God by perfect love, and the will is wholly resigned to Him. Was it not so with the Son of God Himself? Does any child of man endure the distress, the anguish, the agony which He sustained? And yet He knew no sin.

"But can any one who has a pure heart prefer pleasing to unpleasing food; or use any pleasure of sense which is not strictly necessary? If so, how do they differ from others?

"The difference between these and others in taking pleasant food is, (1) They need none of those things to make them happy; for they have a spring of happiness within. They see and love God. Hence they rejoice evermore, and in everything give thanks. (2) They may use them, but they do not seek them. (3) They use them sparingly, and not for the sake of the thing itself. This being premised, we answer directly,—'Such a one may use pleasing food without the danger which attends those who are not saved from sin. He may prefer it to an unpleasing, though equally wholesome food, as a means of increasing thankfulness, with a single eye to God, who giveth us all things richly to enjoy. On the same principle, he may smell to a flower, or eat a bunch of grapes, or take any other pleasure which does not lessen but increase his delight in God. Therefore, neither can we say that one perfected in love would be incapable of marriage, and of worldly business; if he were called thereto, he would be more capable than ever; as being able to do all things without hurry or carefulness, without any distraction of spirit.

"But if two perfect Christians had children, how could they be born in sin, since there was none in the parents?

"It is a possible, but not a probable case. I doubt whether it ever was or ever will be. But waiving this, I answer, 'Sin is entailed upon me, not by immediate generation, but by my first parent.' 'In Adam all died; by the disobedience of one, all men were made sinners;' all men, without exception, who were in his loins when he ate the forbidden fruit.

"We have a remarkable case of this in gardening; grafts on a crab stalk bear excellent fruit; but sow the kernels of this fruit, and what will be the event? They produce as mere crabs as ever were eaten.

"But what does the perfect one do more than others? more than the common believers?

"Perhaps nothing; so may the providence of God have hedged him in by outward circumstances. Perhaps not so much; though he desires and longs to spend and be spent for God, at least, not externally: he neither speaks so many words, nor does so many works. As neither did our Lord Himself speak so many words, or do so many, no nor so great works, as some of His apostles, John xiv. 12. But what then? This is no proof that he has not more grace; and by this God measures the outward work. Hear ye Him: 'Verily, I say unto you, this poor widow has cast in more than them all.' Verily, this poor man, with his few broken words, hath spoken more than them all. Verily, this poor woman, that hath given a cup of cold water, hath done more than them all. Oh, cease to 'judge according to appearance,' and learn to 'judge righteous judgment!'

"But is not this a proof against him,—I feel no power either in his words or prayer?

"It is not: for perhaps that is your own fault. You are not likely to feel any power therein, if any of these hindrances lie in the way: (1) Your own deadness of soul. The dead Pharisees felt no power even in His words who 'spake as never man spake.' (2) The guilt of some unrepented sin lying upon the conscience. (3) Prejudice toward him of any kind. (4) Your not believing that state to be attainable wherein he professes to be. (5) Unreadiness to think or own he has attained it. (6) Overvaluing or idolizing him. (7) Overvaluing yourself and your own judgment. If any of these is the case, what wonder is it that you feel no power in anything he says? But do not others feel it? If they do, your argument falls to the ground. And if they do not, do none of these hindrances lie in their way too? You must be certain of this before you can build any argument thereon; and even then your argument will prove no more than that grace and gifts do not always go together.

" 'But he does not come up to my idea of a perfect Christian.' And perhaps no one ever did, or ever will. For your idea may go beyond; or at least beside the Scriptural account. It may include more than the Bible includes therein, or however, something which does not include. Scripture perfection is, pure love filling the heart, and governing all the words and actions. If your idea includes anything more or anything else, it is not Scriptural; and then no wonder, that a Scripturally perfect Christian does not come up to it.

"I fear many stumble on this stumbling block. They include as many ingredients as they please not according to Scripture but their own imagination, in their idea of one that is perfect; and then readily deny anyone to be such who does not answer that imaginary idea.

"The more care should we take to keep the simple, Scriptural account continually in our eye. Pure love reigning alone in the heart and life,—this is the whole of Scriptural perfection.

"*When may a person judge himself to have attained this?*

"When, after having been convinced of inbred sin, by a far deeper and clearer conviction than that he experienced before justification, and after having experienced a gradual mortification of it, he experiences a total death to sin, and an entire renewal in the love and image of God, so as to rejoice evermore, to pray without ceasing, and in everything to give thanks. Not that 'to feel all love and no sin' is a sufficient proof. Several have experienced this for a time before their souls were fully renewed. None, therefore, ought to believe that the work is done, till there is added the testimony of the Spirit, witnessing his entire sanctification, as clearly as his justification.

"*But whence is it, that some imagine they are thus sanctified when in reality they are not?*

"It is hence; they do not judge by all the preceding marks, but either by part of them, or by others that are ambiguous. But I know no instance of a person attending to them all, and yet deceived in this matter. I believe there can be none in the world. If a man be deeply and fully convinced, after justification, of inbred sin; if he then experience a gradual mortification of sin, and afterward, an entire renewal in the image of God; if to this change, immensely greater than that wrought when he was justified, be added a clear, direct witness of the renewal; I judge it as impossible this man should be deceived herein, as that God should lie. And if one whom I know to be a man of veracity, testify these

61

things to me, I ought not, without some sufficient reason, to reject his testimony.

"Is this death to sin, and renewal in love, gradual or instantaneous?

"A man may be dying for some time; yet he does not, properly speaking, die, till the soul is separated from the body; and in that instant, he lives the life of eternity. In like manner, he may be dying to sin for some time; yet he is not dead to sin, till sin is separated from his soul; and in that instant, he lives the full life of love. And as the change undergone, when the body dies, is of a different kind, and infinitely greater than any we had known before, yea, such as till then, it is impossible to conceive; so the change wrought, when the soul dies to sin, is of a different kind, and infinitely greater than any before, and than any can conceive, till he experiences it. Yet he still grows in grace, in the knowledge of Christ, in the love and image of God; and will do so, not only till death, but to all eternity.

"How are we to wait for this change?

"Not in careless indifference, or indolent inactivity; but in vigorous, universal obedience, in a zealous keeping of all the commandments, in watchfulness and painfulness, in denying ourselves, and taking up our cross daily; as well as in earnest prayer and fasting, and a close attendance on all the ordinances of God. And if any man dream of attaining it any other way (yea, or of keeping it when it is attained, when he has received it even in the largest measure), he deceiveth his own soul. It is true, we receive it by simple faith; but God does not, will not, give that faith, unless we seek it with all diligence, in the way which He hath ordained.

"This consideration may satisfy those who enquire, why so few have received the blessing. Enqire how many are seeking it in this way; and you have a sufficient answer.

"Prayer especially is wanting. Who continues instant therein? Who wrestles with God for this very thing? So, 'ye have not, because ye ask not; or because ye ask amiss,' namely, that you may be renewed before you die. *Before you die!* Will that content you? Nay, but ask that it may be done now; to-day, while it is called to-day. Do not call this 'setting God a time.' Certainly, to-day is His time, as well as to-morrow. Make haste, man, make haste! Let

> *Thy soul break out in strong desire*
> *The perfect bliss to prove;*
> *Thy longing heart be all on fire*
> *To be dissolved in love!*

"*But may we not continue in peace and joy, till we are perfected in love?*

"Certainly we may; for the kingdom of God is not divided against itself; therefore, let not believers be discouraged from 'rejoicing in the Lord always.' And yet we may be sensibly pained at the sinful nature that still remains in us. It is good for us to have a piercing sense of this, and a vehement desire to be delivered from it. But this should only incite us the more zealously to fly every moment to our strong Helper, the more earnestly to 'press forward to the mark, the prize of our high calling in Christ Jesus.' And when the sense of our sin most abounds, the sense of His love should much more abound.

"*How should we treat those who think they have attained?*

"Examine them candidly, and exhort them to pray fervently, that God would show them all that is in their hearts. The most earnest exhortations to abound in every grace, and the strongest cautions to avoid all evil, are given throughout the New Testament, to those who are in the highest state of grace. But this should be done with the utmost tenderness; and without any harshness, sternness, or sourness. We should carefully avoid the very appearance of anger, unkindness, or contempt. Leave it to Satan thus to tempt, and to his children to carry out, 'Let us examine him with despitefulness and torture, that we may know his meekness, and prove his patience.' If they are faithful to the grace given, they are in no danger of perishing thereby; no, not if they remain in that mistake till their spirit is returning to God.

"But what hurt can it do to deal harshly with them?

"Either they are mistaken, or they are not. If they are it may destroy their souls. There is nothing impossible, no, nor improbable. It may so enrage or so discourage them, that they will sink and rise no more. If they are not mistaken, it may grieve those whom God has not grieved, and do much hurt unto our own souls. For, undoubtedly, he that toucheth them, toucheth, as it were, the apple of God's eye. If they are indeed, full of His Spirit, to behave unkindly or contemptuously to them, is doing no little despite to the Spirit of grace. Hereby, likewise, we feed and increase in ourselves evil surmising, and many wrong tempers. To instance only in one: What self-sufficiency is this, to set ourselves up for inquisitors-general, for peremptory judges in these deep things of God! Are we qualified for the office? Can we pronounce, in all cases, how far infirmity reaches? what may, and what may not, be resolved into it? what may, in all circumstances, and what may not, consist with perfect love? Can we precisely determine, how it will influence the look, the gesture, the tone of the voice? If we can, doubtless we are 'the men, and wisdom shall die with us.'

"But if they are displeased at our not believing them, is not this a full proof against them?

"According as that displeasure is. If they are angry, it is a proof against them; if they are grieved, it is not. They ought to be grieved, if we disbelieve a real work of God, and thereby deprive ourselves of the advantage we might have received from it. And we may easily mistake this grief for anger, as the outward expressions of both are much alike.

"But is it not well to find out those who fancy they have attained, when they have not?

"It is well to do it by mild, loving examination. But it is not well to triumph even over these. It is extremely wrong, if we find such an instance, to rejoice as if we had found great spoils. Ought we not rather to grieve, to be deeply concerned, to let our eyes run down with tears? Here is one who seemed to be a living proof of God's power to save to the uttermost; but, alas! it is not as we hoped. He is weighed in the balance, and found wanting! And is this a matter of joy? Ought we not to rejoice a thousand times more, if we can find nothing but pure love?

" 'But he is deceived.' What then? It is a harmless mistake, while he feels nothing but love in his heart. It is a mistake which generally argues great grace, a high degree both of holiness and happiness. This should be a matter of real joy to all that are simple of heart; not the mistake itself, but the height of grace which for a time occasions it. I rejoice that this soul is always happy in Christ, always full of prayer and thanksgiving. I rejoice that he feels no unholy temper, but the pure love of God continually. And I will rejoice, if sin is suspended till it is totally destroyed.

"Is there no danger then in a man's being thus deceived?

"Not at the time that he feels no sin. There was danger before, and there will be again when he comes into fresh trials. But so long as he feels nothing but love animating all his thoughts, and words, and actions, he is in no danger; he is not only happy, but safe, 'under the shadow of the Almighty;' and, for God's sake, let him continue in that love as long as he can. Meantime, you may do well to warn him of danger that will be, if his love grow cold and sin revive; even the danger of casting away hope, and supposing, that because he hath not attained yet, therefore, he never shall.

"But what, if none have attained it yet? What, if all who think so are deceived?

"Convince me of this, and I will preach it no more. But understand me right; I do not build any doctrine on this or that person. This or any other man may be deceived, and I am not moved. But, if there are none made perfect yet, God has not sent me to preach perfection.

"Put a parallel case. For many years I have preached, 'There is a peace of God which passeth all understanding.' Convince me that this word has fallen to the ground; that in all these years none have attained this peace; that there is no living witness of it at this day; and I will preach it no more.

" 'Oh, but several persons have died in that peace.' Perhaps so; but I want living witnesses. I cannot, indeed, be infallibly certain that this or that person is a witness; but if I were certain there are none such, I must have done with this doctrine.

" 'You misunderstand me. I believe some who died in this love, enjoyed it long before their death. But I was not certain that their former testimony was true till some hours before they died.'

"You had not an infallible certainty then: and a reasonable certainty you might have had before; such a certainty as might have quickened and comforted your own soul, and answered all other Christian purpose. Such a certainty as this any candid person may have,

66

suppose there be any living witness, by talking one hour with that person in the love and fear of God.

"But what does it signify whether any have attained it or no, seeing so many scriptures witness for it?

"If I were convinced that none in England had attained what has been so clearly and strongly preached by such a number of preachers, in so many places, and for so long a time, I should be clearly convinced that we had all mistaken the meaning of those Scriptures; and, therefore, for the time to come, I too must teach that 'sin will remain till death.' "

20

The Danger of Fanaticism

In the year 1762, there was a great increase of the work of God in London. Many, who had hitherto cared for none of these things, were deeply convinced of their lost estate; many found redemption in the blood of Christ; not a few blacksliders were healed; and a considerable number of persons believed that God had saved them from all sin. Easily foreseeing that Satan would be endeavoring to sow tares among the wheat, I took much pains to apprize them of the danger, particularly with regard to pride and enthusiasm. And while I stayed in town, I had reason to hope they continued both humble and sober-minded. But almost as soon as I was gone, enthusiasm broke in. Two or three began to take their own imaginations for impressions from God, and thence to suppose that they should never die; and these, laboring to bring others into the same opinion, occasioned much noise and confusion. Soon after, the same persons, with a few more ran into other extravagances; fancying they could not be tempted; that they should feel no more pain; and that they had the gift of prophecy, and of discerning of spirits. At my return to London, in autumn, some of them stood reproved, but others were got above instruction. Meantime, a flood of reproach came upon me almost from every quarter; from themselves, because I was checking them on all occasions; and from others, because they said, I did not check them. However, the hand of the Lord was not stayed, but more and more sinners were convinced; while some were almost daily converted to God, and others enabled to love him with all their heart.

21

Responsibility to Live Above Reproach

About this time, a friend at some distance from London wrote to me as follows: —

"Be not over alarmed that Satan sows tares among the wheat of Christ. It ever has been so, especially on any remarkable outpouring of His Spirit; and ever will be so, till he is chained up for a thousand years. Till then he will always ape, and endeavor to counteract, the work of the Spirit of Christ.

"One melancholy effect of this has been, that a world who is always asleep in the arms of the evil one, has ridiculed every work of the Holy Spirit.

"But what can real Christians do? Why, if they would act worthy of themselves, they should, (1) Pray that every deluded soul may be delivered; (2) Endeavor to reclaim them in the spirit of meekness; and, lastly, take the utmost care, both by prayer and watchfulness, that the delusion of others may not lessen their zeal in seeking after that universal holiness of soul, body, and spirit, 'without which no man shall see the Lord.'

"Indeed, this complete new creature is mere madness to a mad world. But it is, notwithstanding, the will and wisdom of God. May we all seek after it!

"But some who maintain this doctrine in its full extent are too often guilty of limiting the Almighty. He dispenses His gifts just as He pleases; therefore, it is neither wise nor modest to affirm that a person must be a believer for any length of time before he is capable of receiving a high degree of the Spirit of holiness.

"God's usual method is one thing, but His sovereign pleasure is another. He has wise reasons both for hastening and retarding His work. Sometimes He comes suddenly, and unexpected; sometimes, not till we have long looked for Him.

"Indeed, it has been my opinion for many years, that one great cause why men make so little improvement in the Divine life is their own coldness, negligence, and unbelief. And yet I here speak of believers.

"May the Spirit of Christ give us a right judgment in all things, and 'fill us with all the fulness of God;' that so we may be 'perfect and entire, wanting nothing.' "

22

False Ideas on the Second Coming

About the same time, five or six honest enthusiasts foretold the world was to end on the 28th of February. I immediately withstood them, by every possible means, both in public and private. I preached expressly upon the subject both at West Street and Spitalfields. I warned the society, again and again, and spoke severally to as many as I could; and I saw the fruit of my labor. They made exceeding few converts. I believe scarce thirty in our whole society. Nevertheless, they made abundance of noise, gave huge occasion of offense to those who took care to improve to the uttermost every occasion against me, and greatly increased both the number and courage of those who opposed Christian perfection.

23

Questions to Those Who Deny That Christian Perfection Is Attainable in This Life

Some questions now published by one of these, induced a plain man to write the following—

"Queries, humbly proposed to those who deny perfection to be attainable in this life.

" (1) Has there not been a larger measure of the Holy Spirit given under the Gospel, than under the Jewish dispensation? If not, in what sense was the Spirit not given before Christ was glorified? John vii. 39.

" (2) Was that 'glory which followed the sufferings of Christ,' I Peter i. 11, an external glory, or an internal, viz., the glory of holiness?

" (3) Has God anywhere in Scripture commanded us more than He has promised to us?

" (4) Are the promises of God respecting holiness to be fulfilled in this life, or only in the next?

" (5) Is a Christian under any other laws than those which God promises to 'write in our hearts'? Jer. xxxi. 31, etc.; Heb. viii. 10.

" (6) In what sense is 'the righteousness of the law fulfilled in those who walk not after the flesh, but after the Spirit'? Rom. viii. 4.

" (7) Is it impossible for any one in this life to 'love God with all his heart, and mind, and soul, and strength'? And is the Christian under any law which is not fulfilled in this love?

" (8) Does the soul's going out of the body effect its purification from indwelling sin?

" (9) If so, is it not something else, not 'the blood of Christ, which cleanseth' it 'from all sin'?

" (10) If His Blood cleanseth us from all sin, while the soul and body are united, is it not in this life?

" (11) If when that union ceases, is it not in the next? And is not this too late?

" (12) If in the article of death; what situation is the soul in, when it is neither in the body nor out of it?

" (13) Has Christ anywhere taught us to pray for what He never designs to give?

" (14) Has He not taught us to pray, 'Thy will be done on earth, as it is done in heaven?' And is it not done perfectly in heaven?

" (15) If so, has He not taught us to pray for perfection on earth? Does He not then design to give it?

" (16) Did not St. Paul pray according to the will of God, when he prayed that the Thessalonians might be 'sanctified wholly, and preserved' (in this world, not the next, unless he was praying for the dead) 'blameless in body, soul, and spirit, unto the coming of Jesus Christ?'

" (17) Do you sincerely desire to be freed from indwelling sin in this life?

71

"(18) If you do, did not God give you that desire?

"(19) If so, did He not give it you to mock you, since it is impossible it should ever be fulfilled?

"(20) If you have not sincerity enough even to desire it, are you not disputing about matters too high for you?

"(21) Do you ever pray God to 'cleanse the thoughts of your heart, that you may perfectly love Him?'

"(22) If you neither desire what you ask, nor believe it attainable, pray you not as a fool prayeth?

"God help thee to consider these questions calmly and impartially!"

24

The Testimony of Jane Cooper

In the latter end of this year, God called to Himself that burning and shining light, Jane Cooper. As she was both a living and a dying witness of Christian perfection, it will not be at all foreign to the subject to add a short account of her death, with one of her own letters, containing a plain and artless relation of the manner wherein it pleased God to work that great change in her soul: —

May 2, 1761.

"I believe, while memory remains in me, gratitude will continue. From the time you preached on Gal. v. 5, I saw clearly the true state of my soul. That sermon described my heart, and what it wanted to be; namely, truly happy. You read Mr. M—'s letter, and it described

72

the religion which I desired. From that time the prize appeared in view, and I was enabled to follow hard after it. I was kept watching unto prayer, sometimes in much distress, at other time in patient expectation of the blessing. For some days before you left London, my soul was stayed on a promise I had applied to me in prayer: 'The Lord whom ye seek shall suddenly come to His temple.' I believed He would, and that He would sit there as a refiner's fire. The Tuesday after you went, I thought I could not sleep unless He fulfilled His word that night. I never knew, as I did then, the force of these words: 'Be still, and know that I am God.' I became nothing before Him, and enjoyed perfect calmness in my soul. I knew not whether He had destroyed my sin; but I desired to know, that I might praise Him. Yet I soon found the return of unbelief, and groaned, being burdened. On Wednesday, I went to London, and sought the Lord without ceasing. I promised, if He would save me from sin, I would praise Him. I could part with all things, so I might win Christ. But I found all these pleas to be nothing worth; and that if He saved me, it must be freely, for His own name's sake. On Thursday, I was so much tempted that I thought of destroying myself, or never conversing more with the people of God; and yet I had no doubt of His pardoning love; but,—

> 'Twas worse than death my God to love,
> And not my God alone.

On Friday, my distress was deepened. I endeavored to pray, and could not. I went to Mrs. D., who prayed for me, and told me it was the death of nature. I opened the Bible on, 'The fearful and unbelieving shall have their part in the lake which burneth with fire and brimstone.' I could not bear it. I opened again, on Mark xvi. 6, 7: 'Be not affrighted, ye seek Jesus of Nazareth. Go your way; tell His disciples He goeth before you into Galilee; there ye shall see Him,' I was encouraged, and enabled to pray, believing I should see Jesus at home. I returned that night, and found Mrs. G. She prayed for me; and the predestinarian had no plea but, 'Lord, thou art no respecter of persons.' He proved He was not, by blessing me. I was in a moment enabled to lay hold on Jesus Christ, and found salvation by simple faith. He assured me, the Lord, the King, was in the midst of me, and that I should see evil no more. I now blessed Him who had visited and redeemed me, and was become my 'wisdom, righteousness, sanctification, and redemption.' I saw Jesus altogether lovely; and knew He was mine in all His offices. And, glory be to Him, He now reigns in my heart without a rival. I find no will but His. I feel no pride; nor any affection but what is placed on Him. I know it is by faith I stand; and that watching unto prayer must be the guard of faith. I am happy in God this moment, and I believe for the next. I have often read the chapter you mention (1 Cor. xiii), and compared my heart and life with it. In so doing, I feel my shortcomings, and the need I have of the atoning blood. Yet I dare not say I do not feel a measure of the love there described, though I am not all I shall be. I desire to be lost in that 'love which passeth knowledge.' I see 'the just shall live by faith'; and unto me, who am less than the least of all saints, is this grace given. If I were an archangel, I should veil my face before Him, and let silence speak His praise!"

The following account was given by one who was an eye and ear witness of what she relates: —

"(1) In the beginning of November, she seemed to have a foresight of what was coming upon her, and used freqently to sing these words: —

> *When pain o'er this weak flesh prevails,*
> *With lamb-like patience arm my breast.*

And when she sent to me, to let me know she was ill, she wrote in her note, 'I suffer the will of Jesus; all He sends is sweetened by His love. I am as happy as if I heard a voice say: —

> *For me my elder brethren stay,*
> *And angels beckon me away,*
> *And Jesus bids me come!'*

"(2) Upon my telling her, 'I cannot choose life or death for you,' she said, 'I asked the Lord, that, if it was His will, I might die first. And He told me, you should survive me, and that you should close my eyes.' When we perceived it was the smallpox, I said to her, 'My dear, you will not be frightened if we tell you what is your distemper?' She said, 'I cannot be frighted at His will.'

"(3) The distemper was soon very heavy upon her; but so much the more was her faith strengthened. Tuesday, November 16, she said to me, 'I have been worshipping before the throne in a glorious manner; my soul was so let into God!' I said, 'Did the Lord give you any particular promise?' 'No,' replied she; 'it was all

> *That sacred awe that dares not move,*
> *And all the silent heaven of love.'*

"(4) On Thursday, upon my asking, 'What have you to say to me?' she said, 'Nay, nothing but what you know already: God is love.' I asked, 'Have you any particular promise?' She replied, 'I do not seem to want any; I can live without. I shall die a lump of deformity, but shall meet you all glorious: and meantime, I shall still have fellowship with your spirit.'

"(5) Mr. M. asked, what she thought the most excellent way to walk in, and what were its chief hindrances. She answered: 'The greatest hindrance is generally from the natural constitution. It was mine to be reserved, to be very quiet, to suffer much, and to say little. Some may think one way more excellent, and some another; but the thing is to live in the will of God. For some months past, when I have been particularly devoted to this, I have felt such a guidance of His Spirit, and the unction which I have received from the Holy One has so taught me of all things that I needed not any man should teach me, save as this anointing teacheth.'

"(6) On Friday morning she said, 'I believe I shall die.' She then sat up in her bed and said, 'Lord, I bless Thee, that Thou art ever with me, and all Thou hast is mine. Thy love is greater than my weakness, greater than my helplessness, greater than my unworthiness. Lord, Thou sayest *to corruption, Thou art my sister!* And glory be to Thee, O Jesus, Thou art my brother. Let me comprehend, with all saints, the length, and breadth, and depth, and height of Thy love! Bless these' (some that were present); 'let them be every moment exercised in all things as Thou wouldest have them to be.'

"(7) Some hours after, it seemed as if the agonies of death were just coming upon her; but her face was full of smiles of triumph, and she clapped her hands for joy. Mrs. C. said, 'My dear, you are more than conqueror through the blood of the Lamb.' She answered, 'Yes, O yes, sweet Jesus! O death, where is thy sting?' She then lay as in a doze for some time. Afterward, she strove to speak, but could not; however, she testified her love by shaking hands with all in the room.

"(8) Mr. W. then came. She said, 'Sir, I did not know that I should live to see you. But I am glad the Lord has given me this opportunity, and likewise power to speak to you. I love you. You have always preached the strictest doctrine; and I loved to follow it. Do so still, whoever is pleased or displeased.' He asked, 'Do you now believe you are saved from sin?' She said, 'Yes; I have had no doubt of it for many months. That I ever had, was, because I did not abide in the faith.

I now feel I have kept the faith; and perfect love casteth out all fear. As to you, the Lord promised me, your latter works should exceed your former, though I do not live to see it. I have been a great enthusiast, as they term it, these six months; but never lived so near the heart of Christ in my life. You, sir, desire to comfort the hearts of hundreds by following that simplicity your soul loves.'

"(9) To one who had received the love of God under her prayer, she said, 'I feel I have not followed a cunningly devised fable; for I am as happy as I can live. Do you press on, and stop not short of the mark.' To Miss M—s she said, 'Love Christ; He loves you. I believe I shall see you at the right hand of God; but *as one star differs from another star in glory, so shall it be in the resurrection.* I charge you, in the presence of God, meet me in that day all glorious within. Avoid all conformity to the world. You are robbed of many of your privileges. I know I shall be found blameless. Do you labor to be found of Him *in peace, without spot.*'

"(10) Saturday morning, she prayed nearly as follows: 'I know, my Lord, my life is prolonged only to do Thy will. And though I should never eat or drink more' (she had not swallowed anything for near eight-and-twenty hours), 'Thy will be done. I am willing to be kept so a twelve-month; *Man liveth not by bread alone.* I praise Thee that there is not a shadow of complaining in our streets. In that sense we know not what sickness means. Indeed, Lord, *life, nor death, nor things present, nor things to come, no, nor any creature, shall separate us from* Thy *love* one moment. Bless these, that there be no lack in their souls. I believe there shall not. I pray in faith.'

"On Sunday and Monday she was light headed, but sensible at times. It then plainly appeared, her heart was still in heaven. One said to her, 'Jesus is our mark.' She replied: 'I have but one mark; I am all spiritual.'

77

Miss M. said to her, 'You dwell in God.' She answered: 'Altogether.' A person asked her, 'Do you love me?' She said, 'O, I love Christ; I love my Christ.' To another she said, 'I shall not long be here; Jesus is precious, very precious indeed.' She said to Miss M., 'The Lord is very good; He keeps my soul above all.' For fifteen hours before she died, she was in strong convulsions: her sufferings were extreme. One said, 'You are made perfect through sufferings.' She said, 'More and more so.' After lying quiet some time, she said, 'Lord, Thou art strong!' Then pausing a considerable space, she uttered her last words, 'Jesus is all in all to me: glory be to Him through time and eternity.' After this, she lay still for about half an hour and then expired without a sigh or groan."

25

"Farther Thoughts on Christian Perfection"

The law versus love
The fruits of love
What is meant by perfection
The nature of temptation
Possibility of falling
Differences between the justified
    and the sanctified
How to keep sanctified

The next year, the number of those who believed they were saved from sin still increasing, I judged it needful to publish, chiefly for their use,

"Farther Thoughts on Christian Perfection": —

"1. *How is 'Christ the end of the law for righteousness to every one that believeth?'* (Rom. x. 4).

"In order to understand this, you must understand what law is here spoken of; and this, I apprehend, is, (1) The Mosaic law, the whole Mosaic dispensation; which St. Paul continually speaks of as one, though containing three parts, the political, moral, and ceremonial. (2) The Adamic law, that given to Adam in innocence, properly called 'the law of works.' This is in substance the same with the angelic law, being common to angels and men. It required that man should use, to the glory of God, all the powers with which he was created. Now, he was created free from any defect, either in his understanding or his affections. His body was then no clog to the mind; it did not hinder his apprehending all things clearly, judging truly concerning them, and reasoning justly, if he reasoned at all. I say, *if he reasoned;* for possibly he did not. Perhaps he had no need of reasoning, till his corruptible body pressed down the mind, and impaired its native faculties. Perhaps, till then, the mind saw every truth that offered as directly as the eye now sees the light.

"Consequently, this law, proportioned to his original powers, required that he should always think, always speak, and always act precisely right, in every point whatever. He was well able so to do: and God could not but require the service he was able to pay.

"But Adam fell; and his incorruptible body became corruptible; and ever since, it is a clog to the soul, and hinders its operations. Hence, at present, no child of man can at all times apprehend clearly, or judge truly. And where either the judgment or apprehension is wrong, it is impossible to reason justly. Therefore, it is as natural for a man to mistake as to breathe; and he can no more live without the one than without the other: consequently no man is able to perform the service which the Adamic law requires.

"And no man is obliged to perform it; God does not require it of any man; for Christ is the end of the

79

Adamic, as well as the Mosaic, law. By His death He hath puth an end to both; He hath abolished both the one and the other, with regard to man; and the obligation to observe either the one or the other is vanished away. Nor is any man living bound to observe the Adamic more than the Mosaic law. (I mean, it is not the condition either of present or future salvation.)

"In the room of this, Christ hath established another, namely, the law of faith. Not every one that doeth, but every one that believeth, now receiveth righteousness, in the full sense of the word; that is, he is justified, sanctified and glorified.

"2. *Are we then dead to the law?*

"We are 'dead to the law, by the body of Christ' given for us; Rom. vii. 4; to the Adamic as well as Mosaic law. We are wholly freed therefrom by His death; that law expiring with Him.

"3. *How, then, are we 'not without law to God, but under the law to Christ'?* I Cor. ix. 21.

"We are without that law; but it does not follow that we are without any law; for God hath established another law in its place, even the law of faith; and we are all under this law to God and to Christ; both our Creator and our Redeemer require us to observe it.

"4. *Is love the fulfilling of this law?*

"Unquestionably it is. The whole law under which we now are, is fulfilled by love: Rom. xiii. 9, 10. Faith working or animated by love is all that God now requires of man. He has substituted (not sincerity, but) love, in the room of angelic perfection.

"5. *How is 'love the end of the commandment'?* 1 Tim. i. 5.

"It is the end of every commandment of God. It is the point aimed at by the whole and every part of the

Christian institution. The foundation is faith, purifying the heart; and the end love, preserving a good conscience.

"6. *What love is this?*

"The loving the Lord our God with all our heart, mind, soul, and strength; and the loving our neighbor, every man as ourselves, as our own souls.

"7. *What are the fruits or properties of this love?*

"St. Paul informs us at large, love is long-suffering. It suffers all the weaknesses of the children of God, all the wickedness of the children of the world; and that not for a little time only, but as long as God pleases. In all, it sees the hand of God, and willingly submits thereto. Meantime, it is kind. In all, and after all, it suffers, it is soft, mild, tender, benign. 'Love envieth not;' it excludes every kind and degree of envy out of the heart; 'love acteth not rashly,' in a violent, headstrong manner, nor passes any rash or severe judgment; it 'doth not behave itself indecently;' is not rude, does not act out of character; 'seeketh not her own' ease, pleasure, honor, or profit; 'is not provoked;' expels all anger from the heart: 'thinketh no evil;' casteth out all jealousy, suspiciousness, and readiness to believe evil; 'rejoiceth not in iniquity;' yea, weeps at the sin or folly of its bitterest enemies: 'but rejoiceth in the truth;' in the holiness and happiness of every child of man. 'Love covereth all things,' speaks evil of no man; 'believeth all things,' that tend to the advantage of another's character. It 'hopeth all things,' whatever may extenuate the faults which cannot be denied; and it 'endureth all things,' which God can permit, or men and devils inflict. This is the 'law of Christ, the perfect law, the law of liberty.'

"And this distinction between the 'law of faith' (or love) and 'the law of works,' is neither a subtle nor an unnecessary distinction. It is plain, easy, and intelligible to any common understanding. And it is absolutely necessary, to prevent a thousand doubts and fears, even in those who do 'walk in love.'

"8. *But do we not 'in many things offend all,' yea, the best of us, even against this law?*

"In one sense we do not, while all our tempers, and thoughts, and words, and works, spring from love. But in another we do, and shall do, more or less, as long as we remain in the body. For neither love nor the 'unction of the Holy One' makes us infallible: therefore, through unavoidable defect of understanding, we cannot but mistake in many things. And these mistakes will frequently occasion something wrong, both in our temper, and words, and actions. From mistaking his character, we may love a person less than he really deserves. And by the same mistake we are unavoidably led to speak or act, with regard to that person, in such a manner as is contrary to this law in some or other of the preceding instances.

"9. *Do we not then need Christ, even on this account?*

"The holiest of men still need Christ, as their Prophet, as 'the light of the world.' For He does not give them light, but from moment to moment; the instant He withdraws, all is darkness. They still need Christ as their King; for God does not give them a stock of holiness. But unless they receive a supply every moment, nothing but unholiness would remain. They still need Christ as their Priest, to make atonement for their holy things. Even perfect holiness is acceptable to God only through Jesus Christ.

"10. *May not, then, the very best of men adopt the dying martyr's confession: 'I am in myself nothing but sin, darkness, hell; but thou art my light, my holiness, my heaven'?*

"Not exactly. But the best of men say, 'Thou art my light, my holiness, my heaven. Through my union with Thee, I am full of light, of holiness, and happiness. But if I were left to myself, I should be nothing but sin, darkness, hell.'

"But to proceed: The best of men need Christ as their Priest, their Atonement, their Advocate with the Father; not only as the continuance of their every blessing depends on His death and intercession, but on account of their coming short of the law of love. For every man living does so. You who feel all love, compare yourselves with the preceding description. Weigh yourselves in this balance, and see if you are not wanting in many particulars.

"11. *But if all this be consistent with Christian perfection, that perfection is not freedom from all sin; seeing 'sin is the transgression of the law'; and the perfect transgress the very law they are under. Besides, they need the atonement of Christ; and He is the atonement of nothing but sin. Is, then, the term, 'sinless perfection,' proper?*

"It is not worth disputing about. But observe in what sense the persons in question need the atonement of Christ. They do not need Him to reconcile them to God afresh; for they are reconciled. They do not need Him to restore the favor of God, but to continue it. He does not procure pardon for them anew, but 'ever liveth to make intercession for them;' and 'by one offering He hath perfected forever them that are sanctified,' Heb. x. 14.

"For want of duly considering this, some deny that they need the atonement of Christ. Indeed, exceeding few; I do not remember to have found five of them in England. Of the two, I would sooner give up perfection. But we need not give up either one or the other. The perfection I hold, 'Love rejoicing evermore, praying without ceasing, and in everything giving thanks,' is well consistent with it; if any hold perfection which is not, they must look to it.

"12. *Does then Christian perfection imply any more than sincerity?*

"Not if you mean by that word, love filling the heart, expelling pride, anger, desire, self-will; rejoicing evermore, praying without ceasing, and in everything giving thanks. But I doubt, few use sincerity in this sense. Therefore, I think the old word is best.

"A person may be sincere who has natural tempers, pride, anger, lust, self-will. But he is not perfect, till his heart is cleansed from these, and all its other corruptions.

"To clear this point a little farther: I know many that love God with all their heart. He is their one desire, their one delight, and they are continually happy in Him. They love their neighbor as themselves. They feel as sincere, fervent, constant a desire for the happiness of every man, good or bad, friend or enemy, as for their own. They rejoice evermore, pray without ceasing, and in everything give thanks. Their souls are continually streaming up to God, in holy joy, prayer, and praise. This is a point of fact; and this is plain, sound, Scripture experience.

"But even these souls dwell in a shattered body, and are so pressed down thereby, that they cannot always exert themselves as they would, by thinking, speaking, and acting, precisely right. For want of better bodily organs, they must at times think, speak, or act wrong; not, indeed, through a defect of love, but through a defect of knowledge. And while this is the case, notwithstanding that defect, and its consequences, they fulfill the law of love.

"Yet, as even in this case, there is not a full conformity to the perfect law, so the most perfect do, on this very account, need the blood of atonement, and may properly for themselves, as well as for their brethren, say, 'Forgive us our trespasses.'

"13. *But if Christ has put an end to that law, what need of any atonement for their transgressing it?*

"Observe in what sense He has put an end to it, and the difficulty vanishes. Were it not for the abiding merit of His death, and His continual intercession for us, the law would condemn us still. These, therefore, we still need for every transgression of it.

"14. *But can one that is saved from sin be tempted?*

"Yes; for Christ was tempted.

"15. *However what you call temptation, I call the corruption of my heart. And how will you distinguish one from the other?*

"In some cases, it is impossible to distinguish, without the direct witness of the Spirit. But in general, one may distinguish thus: —

"One commends me. Here is a temptation to pride. But instantly my soul is humbled before God. And I feel no pride; of which I am as sure, as that pride is not humility.

"A man strikes me. Here is a temptation to anger. But my heart overflows with love. And I feel no anger at all; of which I can be as sure, as that love and anger are not the same.

"A woman solicits me. Here is a tempation to lust. But in an instant, I shrink back. And I feel no desire or lust at all; of which I can be as sure, as that my hand is cold or hot.

"Thus it is, if I am tempted by a present object; and it is the same, if, when it is absent, the devil recalls a commendation, an injury, or a woman, to my mind. In the instant, the soul repels the temptation, and remains filled with pure love.

"And the difference is still plainer, when I compare my present state with my past, wherein I felt temptation, and corruption too.

85

"*16. But how do you know that you are sanctified, saved from your inbred corruption?*

"I can know it no otherwise than I know that I am justified. 'Hereby know we that we are of God,' in either sense, 'by the Spirit that He hath given us.'

"We know it by the witness and by the fruit of the Spirit. And, First, by the witness. As, when we were justified, the Spirit bore witness with our spirit, that our sins were forgiven; so, when we were sanctified, He bore witness that they were taken away. Indeed, the witness of sanctification is not always clear at first (as neither is that of justification); neither is it afterward always the same, but like that of justification, sometimes stronger, and sometimes fainter. Yea, and sometimes it is withdrawn. Yet, in general, the latter testimony of the Spirit, is both as clear and as steady as the former.

"*17. But what need is there of it, seeing sanctification is a real change, not a relative only, like justification?*

"But is the new birth a relative change only? Is not this a real change? Therefore, if we need no witness of our sanctification, because it is a real change, for the same reason, we should need none, that we are born of, or are, the children of God.

"*18. But does not sanctification shine by its own light?*

"And does not the new birth too? Sometimes it does, and so does sanctification; at others, it does not. In the hour of temptation, Satan clouds the work of God, and injects various doubts and reasonings, especially in those who have either very weak or very strong understandings. At such times, there is absolute need of that witness, without which, the work of sanctification not only could not be discerned, but could no longer subsist. Were it not for this, the soul could not then abide in the love of God; much less could it rejoice evermore, and in every thing give thanks. In these circumstances, therefore, a direct testimony that we are sanctified, is necessary in the highest degree.

"But I have no witness that I am saved from sin. And yet I have no doubt of it. Very well; as long as you have no doubt, it is enough; when you have, you will need that witness.

"19. *But what scripture makes mention of any such thing, or gives any reason to expect it?*

"That scripture, 'We have received, not the spirit that is of the world, but the Spirit which is of God; that we may know the things which are freely given us of God,' 1 Cor. ii. 12.

"Now surely sanctification is one of 'the things which are freely given us of God.' And no possible reason can be assigned why this should be excepted, when the Apostle says, 'We receive the Spirit' for this very end, 'that we may know the things which are' thus 'freely given us.'

"Is not the same thing implied in that well known Scripture, 'The Spirit itself witnesses with our spirit, that we are the children of God'? Rom. viii. 16. Does He witness this only to those who are children of God in the lowest sense? Nay, but to those also who are such in the highest sense. And does He not witness, that they are such in the highest sense? What reason have we to doubt it?

"What if a man were to affirm (as, indeed, many do) that this witness belongs only to the highest class of Christians? Would not you answer, 'The Apostle makes no restriction; therefore, doubtless, it belongs to all the children of God'? And will not the same answer hold, if any affirm, that it belongs only to the lowest class?

"Consider likewise 1 John v. 19: 'We know that

we are of God.' How? 'By the Spirit that He hath given us.' Nay, 'thereby we know that He abideth in us.' And what ground have we, either from Scripture or reason, to exclude the witness, any more than the fruit, of the Spirit, from being here intended? By this, then, also, 'we know that we are of God,' and in what sense we are so; whether we are babes, young men, or fathers, we know in the same manner.

"Not that I affirm that all young men, or even fathers, have this testimony every moment. There may be intermissions, of the direct testimony that they are thus born of God; but these intermissions are fewer and shorter as they grow up in Christ; and some have the testimony both of their justification and sanctification, without any intermission at all; which I presume, more might have, did they walk humbly and closely with God.

"20. *May not some of them have a testimony from the Spirit, that they shall not finally fall from God?*

"They may. And this persuasion, that neither life nor death shall separate them from Him, far from being hurtful, may in some circumstances be extremely useful. These therefore, we should in no wise grieve, but earnestly encourage them to 'hold the beginning of their confidence steadfast to the end.'

"21. *But have any a testimony from the Spirit that they shall never sin?*

"We know not what God may vouchsafe to some particular persons; but we do not find any general state described in Scripture, from which a man cannot draw back to sin, if there were any state wherein this was impossible, it would be that of these who are sanctified, who are 'fathers in Christ, who rejoice evermore, pray without ceasing, and in everything give thanks'; but it is not impossible for these to draw back. They who are sanctified yet may fall and perish: Heb. x. 29.

Even fathers in Christ need that warning: 'Love not the world,' 1 John ii. 15. They who 'rejoice, pray,' and 'give thanks without ceasing,' may, nevertheless, 'quench the Spirit,' 1 Thess. v. 16, etc. Nay, even they who are 'sealed unto the day of redemption,' may yet 'grieve the Holy Spirit of God,' Eph. iv. 3.

"Although, therefore, God may give such a witness to some particular persons, yet it is not to be expected by Christians in general, there being no Scripture whereon to ground such an expectation.

"22. *By what 'fruit of the Spirit,' may we 'know that we are of God,' even in the highest sense?*

"By love, joy, peace, always abiding; by invariable long suffering, patience, resignation; by gentleness, triumphing over all provocation; by goodness, mildness, sweetness, tenderness of spirit; by fidelity, simplicity, godly sincerity; by meekness, calmness, evenness of spirit; by temperance, not only in food and sleep, but in all things natural and spiritual.

"23. *But what great matter is there in this? Have we not all this when we are justified?*

"What! total resignation to the will of God, without any mixture of self-will? gentleness, without any touch of anger, even the moment we are provoked? love to God, without the least love to the creature, but in and for God, excluding all pride? love to man, excluding all envy, all jealousy, and rash judging? meekness, keeping the whole soul inviolably calm? and temperance in all things? Deny that any ever came up to this, if you please; but do not say all who are justified do.

"24. *But some who are newly justified do. What then will we say to these?*

"If they really do, I will say they are sanctified; saved from sin that moment; and that they never need lose what God has given, or feel sin any more.

89

"But certainly this is an exempt case. It is otherwise with the generality of those that are justified; they feel in themselves more or less pride, anger, self-will, a heart bent to backsliding. And, till they have gradually mortified these, they are not fully renewed in love.

"25. *But is not this the case of all that are justified? Do they not gradually die to sin and grow in grace, till at, or perhaps a little before, death, God perfects them in love?*

"I believe this is the case of most, but not all. God usually gives a considerable time for men to receive light, to grow in grace, to do and suffer His will, before they are either justified or sanctified; but He does not invariably adhere to this; sometimes He 'cuts short His work'; He does the work of many years in a few weeks; perhaps in a week, a day, an hour. He justifies or sanctifies both those who have done or suffered nothing, and who have not had time for a gradual growth either in light or grace. And 'may He not do what He will with His own? Is thine eye evil, because He is good?'

"It need not, therefore, be affirmed over and over, and proved by forty texts of Scripture, either that most men are perfected in love at last, that there is a gradual work of God in the soul, or that, generally speaking, it is a long time, even many years, before sin is destroyed. All this we know; but we know likewise, that God may, with man's good leave, 'cut short His work,' in whatever degree He pleases, and do the usual work of many years in a moment. He does so in many instances; and yet there is a gradual work, both before and after that moment; so that one may affirm the work is gradual; another, it is instantaneous, without any manner of contradiction.

"26. *Does St. Paul mean any more by being 'sealed with the Spirit,' than being 'renewed in love'?*

"Perhaps in one place (2 Cor. i. 22), he does not mean so much; but in another (Eph. i. 13), he seems to include both the fruit and the witness; and that in a higher degree than we experience even when we are first 'renewed in love'; God 'sealeth us with the Spirit of promise,' by giving us 'the full assurance of hope'; such a confidence of receiving all the promises of God, as excludes the possibility of doubting; with that Holy Spirit, by universal holiness, stamping the whole image of God on our hearts.

"27. *But how can those who are thus sealed, 'grieve the Holy Spirit of God'?*

"St. Paul tells you very particularly, (1) By such conversation as is not profitable, not to the use of edifying, not apt to minister grace to the hearers. (2) By relapsing into bitterness or want of kindness. (3) By wrath, lasting displeasure, or want of tender-heartedness. (4) By anger, however soon it is over; want of instantly forgiving one another. (5) By clamor or bawling, loud, harsh, rough speaking. (6) By evil speaking, whispering, tale-bearing; needlessly mentioning the fault of an absent person, though in ever so soft a manner.

"28. *What do you think of those in London, who seem to have been lately 'renewed in love'?*

"There is something very peculiar in the experience of the greater part of them. One would expect that a believer should first be filled with love, and thereby emptied of sin; whereas these were emptied of sin first, and then filled with love. Perhaps it pleased God to work in this manner, to make His work more plain and undeniable; and to distinguish it more clearly from that overflowing love which is often felt even in a justified state.

"It seems likewise most agreeable to the great promise; 'From all your filthiness I will cleanse you; a new heart also will I give you, and a new spirit will I put within you,' Ezek. xxxvi. 25, 26.

"But I do not think of them all alike; there is a wide difference between some of them and others. I think most of them with whom I have spoken, have much faith, love, joy and peace. Some of these I believe are renewed in love, and have the direct witness of it; and they manifest the fruit above described, in all their words and actions. Now, let any man call this what he will, it is what I call perfection.

"But some who have much love, peace, and joy, yet have not the direct witness; and others who think they have, are, nevertheless, manifestly wanting in the fruit. How many I will not say; perhaps one in ten; perhaps more or fewer. But some are undeniably wanting in long-suffering, Christian resignation. They do not see the hand of God in whatever occurs, and cheerfully embrace it. They do not in every thing give thanks, and rejoice evermore. They are not happy, at least, not always happy; for sometimes they complain. They say this or that is hard!

"Some are wanting in gentleness. They resist evil, instead of turning the other cheek. They do not receive reproach with gentleness; no, nor even reproof. Nay, they are not able to bear contradiction, without the appearance, at least of resentment. If they are reproved or contradicted, though mildly, they do not take it well; they behave with more distance and reserve than they did before. If they are reproved or contradicted harshly, they answer it with harshness; with a loud voice, or with an angry tone, or in a sharp and surly manner. They speak sharply or roughly, when they reprove others; and behave roughly to their inferiors.

"Some are wanting in goodness. They are not kind, mild, sweet, amiable, soft, and loving at all times, in their spirit, in their words, in their look and air, in the whole tenor of their behavior; and that to all, high and low, rich and poor, without respect of persons; particularly to them that are out of the way, to opposers, and to those of their own household. They do not long, study, endeavor, by every means, to make all about them happy. They can see them uneasy, and not be concerned; perhaps they make them so; and then wipe their mouths and say, 'Why, they deserve it; it is their own fault.'

"Some are wanting in fidelity, a nice regard to truth, simplicity, and godly sincerity. Their love is hardly without dissimulation; something like guile is found in their mouth. To avoid roughness, they lean to the other extreme. They are smooth to an excess, so as scarce to avoid a degree of fawning, or of seeming to mean what they do not.

"Some are wanting in meekness, quietness of spirit, composure, evenness of temper. They are up and down, sometimes high, sometimes low; their mind is not well balanced. Their affections are either not in due proportion; they have too much of one, too little of another; or they are not duly mixed and tempered together, so as to counterpoise each other. Hence there is often a jar. Their soul is out of tune, and cannot make the true harmony.

"Some are wanting in temperance. They do not steadily use that kind of degree of food, which they know, or might know, would most conduce to the health, strength, and vigor, of the body: or they are not temperate in sleep; they do not rigorously adhere to what is best both for body and mind; otherwise they would constantly go to bed and rise early, and at a fixed hour: or they sup late, which is neither good for body nor soul: or they use neither fasting nor abstinence: or they prefer (which are so many sorts of intemperance) that preaching, reading, or conversation, which gives them transient joy and comfort, before that which brings godly sorrow, or instruction in righteousness. Such joy is not sanctified; it doth not tend to, and terminate in, the crucifixion of the heart. Such faith doth not centre in God, but rather in itself.

"So far all is plain. I believe you have faith, and love, and joy and peace. Yet you who are particularly concerned know each for yourself, that you are wanting in the respects above mentioned. You are wanting either in long-suffering, gentleness, or goodness; either in fidelity, meekness, or temperance. Let us not, then, on either hand, fight about words. In the thing we clearly agree.

"You have not what I call perfection; if others will call it so, they may. However, hold fast what you have, and earnestly pray for what you have not.

"29. *Can those who are perfect grow in grace?*

"Undoubtedly they can; and that not only while they are in the body, but to all eternity.

"30. *Can they fall from it?*

"I am well assured they can; matter of fact puts this beyond dispute. Formerly we thought, one saved from sin could not fall; now we know the contrary. We are surrounded with instances of those who lately experienced all that I mean by perfection. They had both the fruit of the Spirit, and the witness; but they have now lost both. Neither does any one stand by virtue of anything that is implied in the nature of the state. There is no such height or strength of holiness as it is impossible to fall from. If there be any that cannot fall, this wholly depends on the promise of God.

"31. *Can those who fall from this state recover it?*

"Why not? We have many instances of this also. Nay, it is an exceeding common thing for persons to lose it more than once, before they are established therein.

94

"It is therefore to guard them who are saved from sin, from every occasion of stumbling, that I give the following advices. But first I shall speak plainly concerning the work itself.

"I esteem this late work to be of God; probably the greatest now upon earth. Yet, like all others, this also is mixed with much human frailty. But these weaknesses are far less than might have been expected; and ought to have been joyfully borne by all that loved and followed after righteousness. That there have been a few weak, warm-headed men, is no reproach to the work itself, no just ground for accusing a multitude of sober-minded men, who are patterns of strict holiness. Yet (just the contrary to what ought to have been) the opposition is great; the helps few. Hereby many are hindered from seeking faith and holiness by the false zeal of others; and some who at first began to run well are turned out of the way.

"32. *What is the First advice that you would give them?*

"Watch and pray continually against pride. If God has cast it out, see that it enter no more; it is full as dangerous as desire. And you may slide back into it unawares; especially if you think there is no danger of it. 'Nay, but I ascribe all I have to God.' So you may, and be proud nevertheless. For it is pride, not only to ascribe anything we have to ourselves, but to thank we have what we really have not. Mr. L——, for instance, ascribed all the light he had to God, and so far he was humble; but then he thought he had more light than any man living; and this was palpable pride. So you ascribe all the knowledge you have to God; and in this respect you are humble. But if you think you have more than you really have; or if you think you are so taught of God, as no longer to need man's teaching; pride lieth at the door. Yes, you have need to be taught,

95

not only by Mr. Morgan, by one another, by Mr. Max-
field, or me, but by the weakest preacher in London;
yea, by all men. For God sendeth by whom he will
send.

"Do not therefore say to any who would advise or
reprove you, 'You are blind; you cannot teach me.' Do
not say, 'This is your wisdom, your carnal reason;' but
calmly weigh the thing before God.

"Always remember, much grace does not imply
much light. These do not always go together. As there
may be much light where there is but little love, so
there may be much love where there is little light.
The heart has more heat than the eye; yet it cannot see.
And God has wisely tempered the members of the body
together, that none may say to another, 'I have no need
of thee.'

"To imagine none can teach you, but those who
are themselves saved from sin, is a very great and
dangerous mistake. Give not place to it for a moment;
it would lead you into a thousand other mistakes, and
that irrecoverably. No; dominion is not founded in
grace, as the madmen of the last age talked. Obey and
regard 'them that are over you in the Lord,' and do not
think you know better than them. Know their place
and your own; always remembering, much love does not
imply much light.

"The not observing this has led some into many
mistakes, and into the appearance at least, of pride.
O beware of the apearance, and the thing! Let 'there
be in you that lowly mind which was in Christ Jesus.'
And 'be ye likewise clothed with humility.' Let it not
only fill, but cover you all over. Let modesty and self-
diffidence appear in all your words and actions. Let all
you speak and do show that you are little, and base,
and mean, and vile in your own eyes.

"As one instance of this, be always ready to own
any fault you have been in. If you have at any time

thought, spoke, or acted wrong, be not backward to acknowledge it. Never dream that this will hurt the cause of God; no, it will farther it. Be, therefore, open, and frank, when you are taxed with anything; do not seek either to evade or disguise it; but let it appear just as it is, and you will thereby not hinder, but adorn the Gospel.

"33. *What is the Second advice which you would give them?*

"Beware of that daughter of pride, enthusiasm. Oh, keep at the utmost distance from it! Give no place to a heated imagination. Do not hastily ascribe things to God. Do not easily suppose dreams, voices, impressions, visions, or revelations to be from God. They may be from Him. They may be from nature. They may be from the devil. Therefore, 'believe not every spirit, but try the spirits whether they be of God.' Try all things by the written word, and let all bow down before it. You are in danger of enthusiasm every hour, if you depart ever so little from Scripture; yea, or from the plain, literal meaning of any text, taken in connection with the context. And so you are, if you despise or lightly esteem reason, knowledge, or human learning; every one of which is an excellent gift of God, and may serve the noblest purposes.

"I advise you, never to use the words, wisdom, reason, or knowledge, by way of reproach. On the contrary, pray that you yourself may abound in them more and more. If you mean worldly wisdom, useless knowledge, false reasoning, say so; and throw away the chaff, but not the wheat.

"One general inlet to enthusiasm is, expecting the end without the means; the expecting knowledge, for instance, without searching the Scriptures, and consulting the children of God; the expecting spritual strength without constant prayer, and steady watchfulness; the expecting any blessing without hearing the word of God at every opportunity.

"Some have been ignorant of this device of Satan. They have left off searching the Scriptures. They said, 'God writes all the Scriptures on my heart. Therefore, I have no need to read it.' Others thought they had not so much need of hearing, and so grew slack in attending the morning preaching. Oh, take warning, you who are concerned herein! You have listened to the voice of a stranger. Fly back to Christ, and keep in the good old way, which was 'once delivered to the saints;' the way that even a heathen bore testimony of, 'That the Christians rose early every day to sing hymns to Christ as God.'

"The very desire of 'growing in grace' may sometimes be an inlet of enthusiasm. As it continually leads us to seek new grace, it may lead us unawares to seek something else new, beside new degrees of love to God and man. So it has led some to seek and fancy they had received gifts of a new kind, after a new heart, as, (1) The loving God with all our mind: (2) With all our soul: (3) With all our strength: (4) Oneness with God: (5) Oneness with Christ: (6) Having our life hid with Christ in God: (7) Being dead with Christ: (8) Rising with Him: (9) The sitting with Him in heavenly places: (10) The being taken up into His throne: (11) The being in the New Jerusalem: (12) The seeing the tabernacle of God come down among men: (13) Te being dead to all works: (14) The not being liable to death, pain, or grief, or temptation.

"One ground of many of these mistakes is, the taking every fresh, strong application of any of these Scriptures to the heart, to be a gift of a new kind; not knowing that several of these Scriptures are not fulfilled yet; that most of the others are fulfilled when we are justified; the rest, the moment we are sanctified.

It remains only to experience them in higher degrees. This is all we have to expect.

"Another ground of these and a thousand mistakes, is, the not considering deeply, that love is the highest gift of God; humble, gentle, patient love; that all visions, revelations, manifestations whatever, are little things compared to love; and that all the gifts above mentioned are either the same with, or infinitely inferior to, it.

"It were well you should be thoroughly sensible of this,—the heaven of heavens is love. There is nothing higher in religion; there is, in effect, nothing else; if you look for anything but more love, you are looking wide of the mark, you are getting out of the royal way. And when you are asking others, 'Have you received this or that blessing?' If you mean anything but more love, you mean wrong; you are leading them out of the way, and putting them upon a false scent. Settle it then in your heart, that from the moment God has saved you from all sin, you are to aim at nothing more, but more of that love described in the thirteenth chapter of the Corinthians. You can go no higher than this, till you are carried into Abraham's bosom.

"I say yet again, beware of enthusiasm. Such is, the imagining you have the gift of prophesying, or discerning of spirits, which I do not believe one of you has; no nor ever had yet. Beware of judging people to be either right or wrong by your own feelings. This is no Scriptural way of judging. Oh, keep close to 'the law and to the testimony!'

"34. *What is the Third?*

"Beware of Antinomianism; 'making void the law,' or any part of it, 'through faith.' Enthusiasm naturally leads to this; indeed, they can scarcely be separated. This may steal upon you in a thousand forms, so that you cannot be too watchful against it. Take heed of everything, whether in principle or practice, which has any tendency thereto. Even that great truth, that 'Christ is the end of the law,' may betray us into it, if we do not consider that He has adoped every point of the moral law, and grafted it into the law of love. Beware of thinking, 'Because I am filled with love, I need not have so much holiness. Because I pray always, therefore I need no set time for private prayer. Because I watch always, therefore I need no particular self-examination.' Let us 'magnify the law,' the whole written word, 'and make it honorable.' Let this be our voice: 'I prize Thy commandments above gold or precious stones. Oh, what love have I unto Thy law! all the day long is my study in it.' Beware of Antinomian books; particularly the works of Dr. Crisp, and Mr. Saltmarsh. They contain many excellent things; and this makes them the more dangerous. Oh, be warned in time! Do not play with fire. Do not put your hand on the hole of a cockatrice' den. I entreat you beware of bigotry. Let not your love or beneficence be confined to Methodists, so-called only; much less to that very small part of them who seem to be renewed in love; or to those who believe yours and their report. Oh, make not this your Shibboleth! Beware of stillness; ceasing in a wrong sense from your own works. To mention one instance out of many: 'You have received,' says one, 'a great blessing. But you began to talk of it, and to do this and that; so you lost it. You should have been still.'

"Beware of self-indulgence; yea, and making a virtue of it, laughing at self-denial, and taking up the cross daily, at fasting or abstinence. Beware of censoriousness; thinking or calling them, that any ways oppose you, whether in judgment or practice, blind, dead, fallen, or 'enemies to the work.' Once more, beware of Solifidianism; crying nothing but 'Believe, believe!' and condemning those as ignorant or legal who speak in a more Scriptural way. At certain seasons, indeed, it may be right to treat of nothing but repentance, or merely of faith, or altogether of holiness; but, in general, our call is to declare the whole counsel of God, and to prophesy according to the analogy of faith. The written word treats of the whole and every particular branch of righteousness, descending to its minutest branches; as to be sober, courteous, diligent, patient, to honor all men. So, likewise, the Holy Spirit works the same in our hearts, not merely creating desires after holiness in general, but strongly inclining us to every particular grace, leading us to every individual part of 'whatsoever is lovely.' And this with the greatest propriety; for us 'by works faith is made perfect,' so the completing or destroying the work of faith, and enjoying the favor, or suffering the displeasure, of God, greatly depends on every single act of obedience or disobedience.

"35. *What is the Fourth?*

"Beware of sins of omission; lose no opportunity of doing good in any kind. Be zealous of good works; willingly omit no work, either of piety or mercy. Do all the good you possibly can, to the bodies and souls of men. Particularly, 'thou shalt in any wise reprove thy neighbor, and not suffer sin upon him.' Be active. Give no place to indolence or sloth; give no occasion to say, 'Ye are idle, ye are idle.' Many will say so still; but let your whole spirit and behavior refute the slander. Be always employed; lose no shred of time; gather up the fragments, that nothing be lost. And whatsoever thy hand findeth to do, do it with thy might. Be 'slow to speak,' and wary in speaking. 'In a multitude of words there wanteth not sin.' Do not talk much; neither long at a time. Few can converse profitably above an hour. Keep at the utmost distance from pious chit-chat, from religious gossiping.

"36. *What is the Fifth?*

"Beware of desiring any thing but God. Now you

desire nothing else; every other desire is driven out; see that none enter again. 'Keep thyself pure;' let your 'eye' remain 'single and your whole body shall be full of light.' Admit no desire of pleasing food, or any other pleasure of sense; no desire of pleasing the eye or the imagination, by any thing grand, or new, or beautiful; no desire of money, of praise, or esteem; of happiness in any creature. You may bring these desires back; but you need not; you need feel them no more. O stand fast in the liberty wherewith Christ hath made you free!

"Be patterns to all of denying yourselves, and taking up your cross daily. Let them see that you make no account of any pleasure which does not bring you nearer to God; nor regard any pain which does; that you simply aim at pleasing Him, whether by doing or suffering; that the constant language of your heart, with regard to pleasure or pain, honor or dishonor, riches or poverty, is,

> All's alike to me, so I
> In my Lord may live and die!"

"37. *What is the Sixth?*

"Beware of schism, of making a rent in the Church of Christ. That inward disunion, the members ceasing to have a reciprocal love 'one for another' (1 Cor. xii. 25), is the very root of all contention, and every outward separation. Beware of every thing tending thereto. Beware of a dividing spirit; shun whatever has the least aspect that way. Therefore, say not, 'I am of Paul, or of Apollos;' the very thing which occasioned the schism at Corinth. Say not, 'This is my preacher; the best preacher in England. Give me him, and take all the rest.' All this tends to breed or foment division, to disunite those whom God hath joined. Do not despise or run down any preacher; do not exalt anyone above the rest, lest you hurt both him and the cause of God. On the other hand, do not bear hard upon any by reason of some incoherency or inaccuracy of expression; no, nor for some mistakes, were they really such.

"Likewise, if you would avoid schism, observe every rule of the society, and of the bands, for conscience' sake. Never omit meeting your class or band; never absent yourself from any public meeting. These are the very sinews of our society; and whatever weakens, or tends to weaken, our regard for these, or exactness in attending them, strikes at the very root of our community. As one saith, 'That part of our economy, the private weekly meetings for prayer, examination, and particular exhoration, has been the greatest means of deepening and confirming every blessing that was received by the word preached, and of diffusing it to others, who could not attend the public ministry; whereas, without this religious connection and intercourse, the most ardent attempts, by mere preaching, have proved of no lasting use.'

"Suffer not one thought of separating from your brethren, whether their opinions agree with yours, or not. Do not dream that any man sins in not believing you, in not taking your word; or that this or that opinion is essential to the work, and both must stand or fall together. Beware of impatience of contradiction. Do not condemn or think hardly of those who cannot see just as you see, or who judge it their duty to contradict you, whether in a great thing, or a small. I fear some of us have thought hardly of others, merely because they contradicted what we affirmed. All this tends to division; and, by every thing of this kind, we are teaching them an evil lesson against ourselves.

"O, beware of touchiness, of testiness, not bearing to be spoken to; starting at the least word; and flying from those who do not implicity receive mine or another's sayings!

"Expect contradiction and opposition, together with crosses of various kinds. Consider the words of St. Paul:

'To you it is given, in the behalf of Christ,'—for His sake, as a fruit of His death and intercession for you,—'not only to believe, but also to suffer for His sake,' Phil. i. 29. It is given! God gives you this opposition or reproach; it is a fresh token of His love. And will you disown the Giver; or spurn His gift, and count it a misfortune? Will you not rather say, 'Father, the hour is come, that Thou shouldest be glorified; now Thou givest Thy child to suffer something for Thee; do with me according to Thy will'? Know that these things, far from being hindrances to the work of God, or to your soul, unless, by your own fault are not only unavoidable in the course of providence, but profitable, yea, necessary for you. Therefore, receive them from God (no from chance), with willingness, with thankfulness. Receive them from men with humility, meekness, yieldingness, gentleness, sweetness. Why should not even your outward appearance and manner be soft? Remember the character of Lady Cutts. 'It was said of the Roman Emperor Titus, Never anyone came displeased from him. But it might be said of her, Never any one went displeased to her; so secure were all of the kind and favorable reception which they would meet with from her.'

"Beware of tempting others, to separate from you. Give no offense which can possibly be avoided; see that your practice be in all things suitable to your profession, adorning the doctrine of God our Saviour. Be particularly careful in speaking of yourself. You may not, indeed, deny the work of God; but speak of it when you are called thereto, in the most inoffensive manner possible. Avoid all magnificent, pompous words; indeed, you need give it no general name; neither perfection, sanctification, the second blessing, nor the having attained. Rather speak of the particulars which God has wrought for you. You may say, 'At such a time, I felt a change which I am not able to express; and since that time, I have not felt pride, or self-will, or anger, or unbelief;

nor any thing but a fulness of love to God and to all mankind.' And answer any other plain question that is asked, with modesty and simplicity.

"And if any of you should at any time fall from what you now are, if you should again feel pride or unbelief, or any temper from which you are now delivered; do not deny, do not hide, do not diguise it at all, at the peril of your soul. At all events, go to one in whom you can confide, and speak just what you feel. God will enable him to speak a word in season, which shall be health to your soul. And surely He will again lift up your head, and cause the bones that have been broken to rejoice.

"38. *What is the last advice that you would give them?*

"Be exemplary in all things; particularly in outward things (as in dress), in little things, in the laying out of your money (avoiding every needless expense), in deep, steady seriousness, and in the solidity and usefulness of all your conversation. So shall you be 'a light shining in a dark place.' So shall you daily grow in grace,' till 'an entrance be ministered unto you abundantly into the everlasting kingdom of our Lord Jesus Christ.'

"Most of the preceding advices are strongly enforced in the following reflections, which I recommend to your deep and frequent consideration, next to the Holy Scriptures: —

" (1) The sea is an excellent figure of the fulness of God, and that of the blessed Spirit. For as the rivers all return into the sea; so the bodies, the souls, and the good works of the righteous, return into God, to live there in His eternal repose.

"Although all the graces of God depend on His mere bounty, yet is He pleased generally to attach them to the prayers, the instructions, and the holiness of those with whom we are. By strong, though invisible attractions, He draws some souls through their intercourse with others.

"The sympathies formed by grace far surpass those formed by nature.

"The truly devout show that passions as naturally flow from true as from false love, so deeply sensible are they of the goods and evils of those whom they love for God's sake. But this can only be comprehended by those who understand the language of love.

"The bottom of the soul may be in repose, even while we are in many outward troubles; just as the bottom of the sea is calm, while the surface is strongly agitated.

"The best helps to growth in grace are the ill-usage, the affronts, and the losses which befall us. We should receive them with all thankfulness, as preferable to all others, were it only on this account,—that our will has not part therein.

"The readiest way to escape from our sufferings is to be willing they should endure as long as God pleases.

"If we suffer persecution and affliction in a right manner, we attain a larger measure of conformity to Christ, by a due improvement of one of these occasions, than we could have done merely by imitating His mercy, in abundance of good works.

"One of the greatest evidences of God's love to those that love Him is to send them afflictions, with grace to bear them.

"Even in the greatest afflictions, we ought to testify to God, that in receiving them from His hand, we feel pleasure in the midst of the pain, from being afflicted by Him who loves us, and whom we love.

"The readiest way which God takes to draw a man to Himself is to afflict him in that he loves most, and with good reason; and to cause this affliction to arise from some good action done with a single eye; because nothing can more clearly show him the emptiness of what is most lovely and desirable in the world.

"(2) True resignation consists in a thorough conformity to the whole will of God, who wills and does all (excepting sin) which comes to pass in the world. In order to do this we have only to embrace all events, good and bad, as His will.

"In the greatest afflictions which can befall the just, either from heaven or earth, they remain immovable in peace, and perfectly submissive to God, by an inward, loving regard to Him, uniting in one all the powers of their souls.

"We ought quietly to suffer whatever befalls us, to bear the defects of others and our own, to confess them to God in secret prayer, or with groans which cannot be uttered; but never to speak a sharp or peevish word, nor to murmur or repine but thoroughly willing that God should treat you in the manner that pleases Him. We are His lambs, and therefore ought to be ready to suffer, even to the death, without compaining.

"We are to bear with those we cannot amend, and to be content with offering them to God. This is true resignation. And since He has borne our infirmities, we may well bear those of each other for His sake.

"To abandon all, to strip one's self of all, in order to seek and to follow Jesus Christ naked to Bethlehem, where He was born; naked to the hall where He was scourged; and naked to Calvary, where He died on the cross, is so great a mercy, that neither the thing, nor the knowledge of it, is given to any, but through faith in the Son of God.

"(3) There is no love of God without patience, and no patience without lowliness and sweetness of spirit.

"Humility and patience are the surest proofs of the increase of love.

"Humility alone unites patience with love, without which it is impossible to draw profit from suffering, or, indeed, to avoid complaint, especially when we think we have given no occasion for what men make us suffer.

"True humility is a kind of self-annihilation, and this is the centre of all virtues.

"A soul returned to God ought to be attentive to everything which is said to him, on the head of salvation, with a desire to profit thereby.

"Of the sins which God has pardoned, let nothing remain but a deeper humility in the heart, and a stricter regulation in our words, in our actions, and in our sufferings.

"(4) The bearing men, and suffering evils in meekness and silence, is the sum of a Christian life.

"God is the first object of our love: its next office is, to bear the defects of others. And we should begin the practice of this amidst our own household.

"We should chiefly exercise our love toward them who most shock either our way of thinking, or our temper, or our knowledge, or the desire we have that others should be as virtuous as we wish to be ourselves.

"(5) God hardly gives His Spirit even to those whom He has established in grace, if they do not pray for it on all occasions, not only once, but many times.

"God does nothing but in answer to prayer; and even they who have been converted to God, without praying for it themselves (which is exceeding rare), were not without the prayers of others. Every new victory which a soul gains is the effect of a new prayer.

"On every occasion of uneasiness, we should retire to prayer, that we may give place to the grace and light of God, and then form our resolutions, without being in any pain about what success they may have.

"In the greatest temptations, a single look to Christ, and the barely pronouncing His name, suffices to overcome the wicked one, so it be done with confidence and calmness of spirit.

"God's command to 'pray without ceasing,' is founded on the necessity we have of His grace to preserve the life of God in the soul, which can no more subsist one moment without it, than the body can without air.

"Whether we think of, or speak to, God, whether we act or suffer for Him, all is prayer, when we have no other object than His love, and the desire of pleasing Him.

"All that a Christian does, even in eating and sleeping, is prayer, when it is done in simplicity, according to the order of God, without either adding to or diminishing from it by his own choice.

"Prayer continues in the desire of the heart, though the understanding be employed on outward things.

"In souls filled with love, the desire to please God is a continual prayer.

"As the furious hate which the devil bears us is termed the roaring of a lion, so our vehement love may be termed crying after God.

"God only requires of His adult children, that their hearts be truly purified, and that they offer Him continually the wishes and vows that naturally spring from perfect love. For these desires, being the genuine fruits of love, are the most perfect prayers that can spring from it.

" (6) It is scarce conceivable how straight the way is wherein God leads them that follow Him; and how dependent on Him we must be, unless we are wanting in our faithfulness to Him.

"It is hardly credible of how great consequence before God the smallest things are; and what great inconveniences sometimes follow those which appear to be light faults.

"As a very little dust will disorder a clock, and the least sand will obscure our sight, so the least grain of sin which is upon the heart will hinder its right motion toward God.

"We ought to be in the church as the saints are in heaven, and in the house as the holiest men are in the church; doing our work in the house as we pray in the church; worshipping God from the ground of the heart.

"We should be continually laboring to cut off all the useless things that surround us; and God usually retrenches the superfluities of our souls in the same proportion as we do those of our bodies.

"The best means of resisting the devil is, to destroy whatever of the world remains in us, in order to raise for God, upon its ruins, a building all of love. Then shall we begin, in this fleeting life, to love God as we shall love Him in eternity.

"We scarce conceive how easy it is to rob God of His due, in our friendship with the most virtuous persons, until they are torn from us by death. But if this loss produce lasting sorrow, that is a clear proof that we had before two treasures, between which we divided our heart.

" (7) If, after having renounced all, we do not watch incessantly, and beseech God to accompany our vigilance with His, we shall be again entangled and overcome.

"As the most dangerous winds may enter at little openings, so the devil never enters more dangerously than by little unobserved incidents, which seem to be nothing, yet insensibly open the heart to great temptations.

"It is good to renew ourselves from time to time, by closely examining the state of our souls, as if we had never done it before: for nothing tends more to the full assurance of faith, than to keep ourselves by this means in humility, and the exercise of all good works.

"To continual watchfulness and prayer ought to be added continual employment. For grace flies a vacuum as well as nature; and the devil fills whatever God does not fill.

"There is no faithfulness like that which ought to be between a guide of souls and the person directed by Him. They ought continually to regard each other in God, and closely to examine themselves, whether all their thoughts are pure, and all their words directed with Christian discretion. Other affairs are only the things of men; but these are peculiarly the things of God.

" (8) The words of St. Paul, 'No man can call Jesus Lord, but by the Holy Ghost,' show us the necessity of eyeing God in our good works, and even in our minutest thoughts; knowing that none are pleasing to Him, but those which He forms in us and with us. From hence we learn that we cannot serve Him, unless He use our tongue, hands, and heart, to do by Himself and His Spirit whatever He would have us to do.

"If we were not utterly impotent, our good works would be our own property; whereas now they belong wholly to raising our works, and making them all Divine, He honors Himself in us through them.

"One of the principal rules of religion is, to lose no occasion of serving God. And, since He is invisible to our eyes, we are to serve Him in our neighbor; which He receives as if done to Himself in person, standing visibly before us.

"God does not love men that are inconstant, nor good works that are intermitted. Nothing is pleasing to

Him, but what has a resemblance of His own immutability.

"A constant attention to the work which God entrusts us with is a mark of solid piety.

"Love fasts when it can, and as much as it can. It leads to all the ordinances of God, and employs itself in all the outward works whereof it is capable. It flies, as it were, like Elijah over the plain, to find God upon His holy mountain.

"God is so great, that He communicates greatness to the least thing that is done for His service.

"Happy are they who are sick, yea, or lose their life, for having done a good work.

"God frequently conceals the part which His children have in the conversion of other souls. Yet one may boldly say, that person who long groans before Him for the conversion of another, whenever that soul is converted to God, is one of the chief causes of it.

"Charity cannot be practiced right, unless, First, we exercise it the moment God gives the occasion; and, Secondly, retire the instant after to offer it to God by humble thanksgiving. And this for three reasons: First, to render Him what we have received from Him. The Second, to avoid the dangerous temptation which springs from the very goodness of these works. And the Third, to unite ourselves to God, in whom the soul expands itself in prayer, with all the graces we have received, and the good works we have done, to draw from Him new strength against the bad effects which these very works may produce in us, if we do not make use of the antidotes which God has ordained against these poisons. The true means to be filled anew with the riches of grace is thus to strip ourselves of it; and without this it is extremely difficult not to grow faint in the practice of good works.

"Good works do not receive their last perfection, till they, as it were, lose themselves in God. This is a kind of death to them, resembling that of our bodies, which will not attain their highest life, their immortality, till they lose themselves in glory of our souls, or rather of God, wherewith they shall be filled. And it is only what they had of earthly and mortal, which good works lose by this spiritual death.

"Fire is the symbol of love; and the love of God is the principle and the end of all our good works. But truth surpasses figure; and the fire of Divine love has this advantage over material fire, that it can reascend to its source, and raise thither with it all the good works which it produces. And by this means it prevents their being corrupted by pride, vanity, or any evil mixture. But this cannot be done otherwise than by making these good works in a spiritual manner die in God, by a deep gratitude, which plunges the soul in Him as in an abyss, with all that it is, and all the grace and works for which it is indebted to Him; a gratitude, whereby the soul seems to empty itself of them, that they may return to their source, as rivers seem willing to empty themselves, when they pour themselves with all their waters into the sea.

"When we have received any favor from God, we ought to retire, if not into our closets, into our hearts, and say, 'I come, Lord, to restore to Thee what Thou hast given; and I freely relinquish it, to enter again into my own nothingness. For what is the most perfect creature in heaven or earth in Thy presence, but a void capable of being filled with Thee and by Thee; as the air which is void and dark, is capable of being filled with the light of the sun, who withdraws it every day to restore it the next, there being nothing in the air that either appropriates this light or resists it? O give me the same facility of receiving and restoring Thy grace and good works! I say, Thine; for I acknowledge the root from which they spring is in Thee, and not in me.' "

26

Brief Summation of Wesley's Views

In the year 1764, upon a review of the whole subject, I wrote down the sum of what I had observed in the following short propositions: —

"(1) There is such a thing as perfection; for it is again and again mentioned in Scripture.

"(2) It is not so early as justification; for justified persons are to 'go on unto perfection,' Heb. vi. 1.

"(3) It is not so late as death; for St. Paul speaks of living men that were perfect, Phil. iii. 15.

"(4) It is not absolute. Absolute perfection belongs not to man, nor to angels, but to God alone.

"(5) It does not make any man infallible; none is infallible, while he remains in the body.

"(6) Is it sinless? It is not worth while to contend for a term. It is 'salvation from sin.'

"(7) It is 'perfect love,' 1 John iv. 18. This is the essence of it; its properties, or inseparable fruits, are, rejoicing evermore, praying without ceasing, and in every thing giving thanks, 1 Thess. v. 16, etc.

"(8) It is improvable. It is so far from lying in an indivisible point, from being incapable of increase, that one perfected in love may grow in grace far swifter than he did before.

"(9) It is amissible, capable of being lost; of which we have numerous instances. But we were not thoroughly convinced of this, till five or six years ago.

"(10) It is constantly both preceded and followed by a gradual work.

"(11) But is it in itself instantaneous or not? In examining this, let us go on step by step.

"An instantaneous change has been wrought in some believers. None can deny this.

"Since that change, they enjoy perfect love; they feel this, and this alone; they 'rejoice evermore, pray without ceasing, and in everything give thanks.' Now this is all that I mean by perfection; therefore, these are witnesses of the perfection which I preach.

" 'But in some, this change was not instantaneous.' They did not perceive the instant when it was wrought. It is often difficult to perceive the instant when a man dies; yet there is an instant in which life ceases. And if ever sin ceases, there must be a last moment of its existence, and a first moment of our deliverance from it.

" 'But if they have this love now, they will lose it.' They may; but they need not. And whether they do or no, they have it now; they now experience what we teach. They now are all love; they now rejoice, pray, and praise without ceasing.

" 'However sin is only suspended in them; it is not destroyed.' Call it which you please. They are all love today; and they take no thought for the morrow.

" 'But this doctrine has been much abused.' So has that of justification by faith. But that is no reason for giving up either this or any other Scriptural doctrine. 'When you wash your child,' as one speaks, 'throw away the water; but do not throw away the child.'

" 'But those who think they are saved from sin, say they have no need of the merits of Christ.' They say just the contrary. Their language is, —

> *Every moment, Lord, I want,*
> *The merit of Thy death!*

"They never before had so deep, so unspeakable a conviction of the need of Christ in all His offices, as they have now.

"Therefore, all our preachers should make a point of preaching perfection to believers, constantly, strongly and explicity; and all believers should mind this one thing, and continually agonize for it."

27

Plea for Impartial Judgment of His Teaching

I have now done what I proposed. I have given a plain and simple account of the manner wherein I first received the doctrine of perfection, and the sense wherein I received, and wherein I do receive, and teach it to this day. I have declared the whole and every part of what I mean by that Scriptural expression. I have drawn the picture of it at full length, without either disguise or covering.

And I would now ask any impartial person, What is there so frightful therein? Whence is all this outcry, which, for these twenty years and upwards, has been made throughout the kingdom; as if all Christianity were destroyed, and all religion torn up by the roots? Why is it, that the very name of perfection has been cast out of the mouths of Christians; yea, exploded and abhorred, as if it contained the most pernicious heresy? Why have the preachers of it been hooted at, like mad dogs, even by men that fear God; nay, and by some of their own children, some whom they, under God, had begotten through the Gospel? What reason is there for this, or what pretence? Reason, sound reason, there is none. It is impossible there should. But pretences there are, and those in great abundance. Indeed, there is ground to fear that, with some who treat us thus, it is mere pretense; that it is no more than a copy of their countenance, from the beginning to the end. They wanted, they sought occasion against me; and here they found what they sought. "This is Mr. Wesley's doctrine! He preaches perfection!" He does; yet this is not his doctrine, anymore than it is yours, or anyone's else, that is a minister of Christ. For it is His doctrine, peculiarly, emphatically His; it is the doctrine of Jesus Christ. Those are His words, not mine: "Ye shall therefore be perfect, as your Father who is in heaven, is perfect." And who says, ye shall not; or at least, not till your soul is separated from the body?

It is the doctrine of St. Paul, the doctrine of St. James, of St. Peter, and St. John; and no otherwise Mr. Wesley's, than as it is the doctrine of every one who preaches the pure and the whole Gospel. I tell you, as plain as I can speak, where and when I found this. I found it in the oracles of God, in the Old and New Testament; when I read them with no other view or desire, but to save my own soul. But whosesoever this doctrine is, I pray you, what harm is there in it?

Look at it again; survey it on every side, and that with the closest attention. In one view, it is purity of intention, dedicating all the life to God. It is the giving God all our heart; it is one desire and design ruling all our tempers. It is the devoting, not a part, but all, our soul, body, and substance, to God. In another view, it is all the mind which was in Christ, enabling us to walk as Christ walked. It is the circumcision of the heart from all filthiness, all inward as well as outward pollution. It is a renewal of the heart in the whole image of God, the full likeness of Him that created it. In yet another, it is the loving God with all our heart, and our neighbor as ourselves. Now, take it in which of these views you please (for there is no material difference), and this is the whole and sole perfection, as a train of writings prove to a demonstration, which I have believed and taught for these forty years, from the year 1725 to the year 1765.

28

A Defense of the Doctrine

Now let this perfection appear in its native form, and who can speak one word against it? Will any dare to speak against loving the Lord our God with all our heart, and our neighbor as ourselves? against a renewal of heart, not only in part, but in the whole image of God? Who is he that will open his mouth against being cleansed from all pollution both of flesh and spirit; or against having all the mind that was in Christ, and walking in all things as Christ walked? What man, who calls himself a Christian, has the hardiness to object to the devoting, not a part, but all our soul, body, and substance to God? What serious man would oppose the giving God all our heart, and the having one desire ruling all our tempers? I say again, let this Christian perfection appear in its own shape, and who will fight against it? It must be disguised before it can be opposed. It must be covered with a bearskin first, or even the wild beasts of the people will scarce be induced to worry it.

But whatever these do, let not the children of God any longer fight against the image of God. Let not the members of Christ say anything against the whole mind that was in Christ. Let not those who are alive to God oppose the dedicating all our life to Him. Why should you who have His love shed abroad in your heart, withstand the giving Him all your heart? Does not all that is within you cry out, "Oh, who that loves can love enough?' What pity that those who desire and design to please Him should have any other design or desire! Much more that they should dread, as a fatal delusion, yea, abhor as an abomination to God, the having this one desire and design ruling every temper!

Why should devout men be afraid of devoting all their soul, body, and substance to God? Why should those who love Christ count it a damnable error to think we may have all the mind that was in Him? We allow, we contend, that we are justified freely through the righteousness and the blood of Christ.

And why are you so hot against us, because we expect likewise to be sanctified wholly through His Spirit? We look for no favor either from the open servants of sin, or from those who have only the form of religion. But how long will you who worship God in spirit, who are "circumcised with the circumcision not made with hands," set your battle in array against those who seek an entire circumcision of heart, who thirst to be cleansed "from all filthiness of flesh and spirit," and to "perfect holiness in the fear of God"?

Are we your enemies because we look for a full deliverance from the "carnal mind which is enmity against God"? Nay, we are your brethren, your fellow-laborers in the vineyard of our Lord, your companions in the kingdom and patience of Jesus. Although this we confess (if we are fools therein, yet as fools bear with us), we do expect to love God with all our heart, and our neighbor as ourselves. Yea, we do believe that He will in this world so "cleanse the thoughts of our hearts by the inspiration of His Holy Spirit, that we shall perfectly love Him, and worthily magnify His holy name."

119